MEMORIE
OF
BIRMINGHAM

ALTON DOUGLAS
DENNIS MOORE
ADDITIONAL RESEARCH BY
JO DOUGLAS

© 1986 ALTON DOUGLAS, DENNIS MOORE, JO DOUGLAS
© 1996 ALTON AND JO DOUGLAS
14TH IMPRESSION
Published by Brewin Books, Doric House, Church Street, Studley, Warwickshire. B80 7LG.
Printed by Heron Press, 19 Bilton Ind. Est., Kings Norton, Birmingham B38 9TS.
ISBN No. 0 947731 81 4

CONTENTS

c/o Brewin Books,
Doric House, Church Street,
Studley,
Warks. B80 7LG.

Dear Nostalgic,

I just wanted to have a brief word with you before you drift off into the atmosphere of a world that only old photographs can create. It has proved to be absorbing to concentrate again on my home town in this, our ninth book (nine! It doesn't seem possible after just five short years!). But I wonder if you'll experience the same emotions that I did as you go back into times that are seldom accurately remembered? Gratitude - as you realise how Joseph Chamberlain's achievements enriched our city; the debt we owe to the Martineau family as this year they provide us with a fifth "First Citizen"; indeed, so many heroes and heroines who contributed to make Birmingham such a great place. Frustration - as you look at treasured long-lost buildings and realise that countless committees have been guilty of far more acts of vandalism than all of today's youngsters. Fascination - as you look into the thousands of faces gathered to greet you and realise that they experienced all the same pleasures and trials that we feel are unique.

Don't expect to find reams of facts and figures: this is not intended to be an in-depth history book but rather a series of random dips into the past. Possibly, if something in it sparks off your imagination, it will point you in the direction of further research and I know, from personal experience, how enjoyable that can be.

Dennis, Jo and I would like to thank everyone involved, with such good-humoured patience, in the preparation of this book. In particular we would like to thank Clive Hardy, who has been responsible for the layout of all our books so far and Gordon Stretch, who painstakingly ensures that we dot our t's and cross our i's (you see no-one is perfect!).

In closing, I do hope that somewhere in these pages you find at least one of your favourite images preserved forever. Happy searching!

Yours in friendship,

Alton

ALTON DOUGLAS is probably best known as the author of several best-selling books and for the three years he was quizmaster (and co-writer) of the top-rated BBC Midlands TV series "Know Your Place". However, he is also a TV and radio character actor, ex-professional comedian, showbiz/jazz book and record reviewer, TV and radio commercial voice-over artist, one-time 5th Royal Inniskilling Dragoon Guards trombonist, the voice behind several cartoons and children's toys, etc.

He has appeared in virtually every major theatre in the U.K. (including the London Palladium) and was responsible for hundreds of television studio warm-ups.

His television appearances include "Know Your Place" (3 series), "Angels", "Seconds Out", "A Soft Touch", "Muck and Brass", "The Golden Shot", "The Knockers", "The Original Alton Douglas", "Nights at the Swan", "Watch This Space", "The Barmaid's Arms", "Open University", "Property Rites", "Big Deal", "Newshound", "Murder of a Moderate Man" and "The Bretts". His radio plays include "Mr Peabody and the Beast", "Troupers", "The Family That Plays Together, Stays Together", "You Can't Judge a Book by Looking at the Cover", "Sorry Goodbye and Get Stuffed" and the award-winning "Guernica". He was also the archives and stills consultant for the centenary video "Made in Birmingham".

Since 1981 Alton has had over two dozen books published:
"Birmingham in the Fifties"
"Birmingham in the Sixties"
"Birmingham: A Look Back"
"Birmingham Remembered"
"Memories of Birmingham"
"Birmingham at Play"
"Birmingham Shops"
"Birmingham at Work"
"Birmingham: The War Years"
"Birmingham at War Vol 1"
"Birmingham at War Vol 2"
"Dogs in Birmingham"
"Coventry: A Century of News"
"Memories of Coventry"
"Coventry at War"
"Memories of Stratford-upon-Avon"
"Joe Russell's Smethwick"
"The Black Country Remembered"
"Memories of the Black Country"
"The Black Country at Play"
"The Black Country at War"
"Memories of Dudley"
"Memories of Walsall"
"Memories of West Bromwich"
"Memories of Wolverhampton"
"Memories of Shrewsbury"
"Memories of the Wrekin and Beyond"
"Alton Douglas's Celebrity Recipes"
"Alton Douglas's Know Your Place"

*** LOOK OUT FOR NEW TITLES EACH YEAR ***

INTRODUCTION

The Domesday Book (1083-1086) set out an objective of making everyone who owned land pay towards the defence of the country according to the number of acres held and their worth. The Book said: "Richard de Bermingeham holds of William Fitz-Ausculf four hides (480 acres) in Bermingham. The arable employs six ploughs. There are four villeins (sharers in the common land) and two ploughs. A wood half a mile long and four furlongs broad. Its worth is 20 shillings (£1)."

From the above extract it will be noticed that the spelling of Birmingham varied even in the same sentence. The name has been spelt in 140 different ways.

Birmingham is a thoroughly Saxon name and seems to have been derived like this:

BERM (or BEORM)	– a family or tribe name.
ING (or IUNG)	– the young or progeny of a tribe.
HAM	– home or residence.
Hence, Birmingham	– the home of the young of the Berm family.

Peter de Bermingham held the manor in 1166 and had his castle "scarce a bow's shot from the church, south-westward." The church, of course, was the original St Martin's and the castle-moat gave rise to Moat Row and Moat Lane near the Smithfield (wholesale fruit) Market. The early township consisted of 3,000 acres (today it covers 65,000 acres) with twelve ancient parishes, viz. Sutton Coldfield, Minworth, Handsworth, Aston, Birmingam, Edgbaston, Yardley, Sheldon, Harborne, Quinton, Northfield and Kings Norton.

In 1841 the population was 182, 894; in 1851, 232,841; in 1861, 296, 076; in 1931, 1,002,413; and by the summer of 1986 the figure was approximately 1,012,900.

Post Office statistics show how the city has grown:
In 1886, 13,023,200 letters were delivered. There were 9 Post Offices, 60 post boxes and 162 employees. By 1886 these had risen to 30,983,625 letters, 33 P.O.'s, 233 boxes and 868 employees. In 1985 the figures were: 384,076,000 letters, 447 P.O.'s, 2,191 boxes and 5,761 employees.

Such progress came about because of Birmingham's emergence as a centre of industrial diligence, brilliant design and superb inventions. At the source were Matthew Boulton and James Watt. Boulton was born in the city and lived in Snow Hill. He enlarged his father's silver stamping factory near St Michael's Church, Handsworth, employing hundreds of people. His house is still near the site of the old works and he is buried, like his friend Watt, at Handsworth. James Watt, a Scot, adopted Birmingham as the city adopted him, and, with Boulton perfected an experimental engine embodying the essential features of the modern steam-engine.

The Birmingham Canal (completed in 1769) was an important transport and freight system and even today is the centre of the country's canal system.

Newspapers came early in Birmingham's history. Warren's Journal, to which Dr Johnson was a contributor, had come and gone by 1732, but the Birmingham Gazette opened in 1741, pre-dating even The Times by 44 years. The Birmingham Daily Post was launched in 1857.

Having been granted a Charter of Incorporation in 1838, Birmingham became a city in 1889 and created its first Lord Mayor in 1896.

Famous men and women (too many for all to be recorded here) have graced the city's scene. To Joseph Chamberlain goes the accolade of creator of a beautiful city centre. In his conception of a new thoroughfare, Corporation Street, to link New Street to Aston Road, he wished to establish an avenue as broad and as handsome as a Parisian boulevard. In the process, he was able to wipe away some of the worst slums and undesirable areas of the city, for example around the Old Square, Lichfield Street and Staniforth Street. Such was municipal progress at that time that even American opinion was that Birmingham was "the best governed city in the world".

Neville Chamberlain, Joseph's son, although an ardent peace-lover, as Prime Minister led his country to war in 1939 at least with a united nation behind him. He had earlier, in 1935, approved plans for the production of the Spitfire (at Castle Bromwich) and the Hurricane aircraft which won the Battle of Britain in 1940 and paved the way for eventual victory. Other well-known families and individuals are commemorated by named districts and roads, for example the Calthorpes, Smallbrokes and Colmores. There are indeed many more.

On very early maps of the Midlands even Dudley was seen to be a bigger town, yet for a long time Birmingham has been Britain's Second City, bearing her motto, "Forward", with pride.

Of the many ways of spelling Birmingham, "Bromwycham" or "Bromicham" are examples. How easy, then, to corrupt these to "Brummagem". Earlier, sadly, a "Brummagem job" had unfortunate connotations, meaning as it did, "a poor or unsatisfactory product or undertaking." Happily, due to the dedication and skill of the city's workers, architects and administrators, this label has now been destroyed.

In any developing community, shops and offices inevitably take over sites of earlier, often dissimilar, businesses. Shop-fronts, in new materials and modern styles, tend to obscure the memory of what was there before. In your journeys on foot around the city centre or your local district, pause and raise your eyes above first floor level. There, as often as not, the upper parts of the buildings will surprise you, for revealed will be many reminders of your old Birmingham, the Birmingham perhaps of your youth, the Birmingham you believed had gone forever.

No. 51.—Vol XLII.   BIRMINGHAM, JULY 6, 1901.   [One Penny.

THE TOWN CRIER.
Or, Jacob's Belles Lettres.

5

BEGINNINGS

The city could boast some very fine grammar schools, yet it was also served well by schools in the poor districts. Gas lighting was common to all grades of school and, in some infants' schools, guarded, open coal-fires formed a focal point when storytime came around.

The Hazelwood School, frankly experimental, was sited opposite the Portland Road junction at 146-150, Hagley Road, Edgbaston. Erected in 1819, it had been designed by Mr (later Sir) Rowland Hill, the pioneer of the "penny post". School committees were set up to manage its own affairs; internal courts of justice were inaugurated; all types of corporal punishment were abolished; there were incentives and rewards to improve standards; regular, organ- ised games were compulsory each afternoon. Its firm rules and discipline were such that the American penitentiary, Sing Sing (the prison so often portrayed in films) adopted many of its ideas as suitable to its own needs! Late in its existence, the Edgbaston landmark became a hotel and an office of the Ministry of National Insurance (as it was then). A decision to demolish was taken late in 1960 and the work was carried out soon afterwards.

In 1772 the Blue Coat School was established "to provide practical education for poor but respectable children with emphasis on reading, writing and an interest in Christian fellowship."

Another experiment was the Billesley Council School of 1925 with its open-air classrooms fitted with screens leading onto verandahs deep enough to shade the pupils from the glare of the sun. In winter, heating came from the pipes beneath the floor. By 1978 Birmingham could be proud of some 500 schools, excluding "specials".

Youth organisations always seemed to flourish. In Birmingham the Boys' Brigade began in 1902, the Boy Scouts in 1908, the Girl Guides in 1909 and the Birmingham Federation of Boys' Clubs in 1928.

St George's C. of E. School, Great Russell Street, Newtown, 1881.

Dennis Road School, Balsall Heath, 1896.

Stirchley Street School, c. 1903. Stirchley Street is now known as Pershore Road.

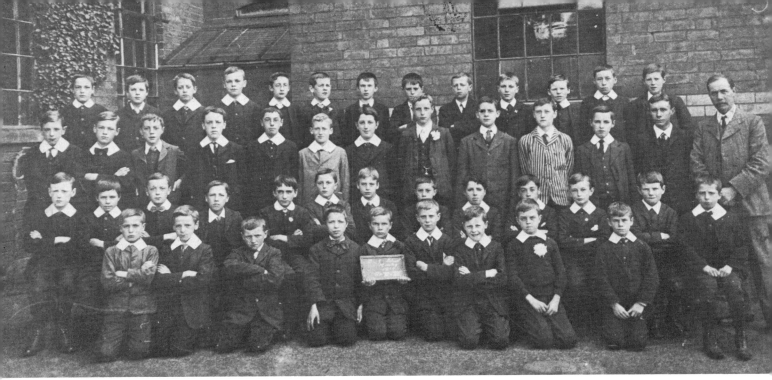

C. of E. School, School Road, Moseley, 1912.

Kingsvale School, Kingstanding Road, 1922.

The "new" King Edward's Grammar School for Girls, Rosehill Road, Handsworth, July 1911.

Hawthorn Road Junior School, Perry Common, 1929. The curtain was used to divide two classes.

Sladefield Road School, Ward End, 1932.

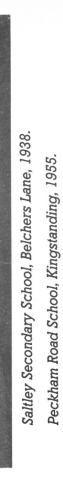

Saltley Secondary School, Belchers Lane, 1938.

Peckham Road School, Kingstanding, 1955.

St Anne's R.C. School, Alcester Street, Deritend, 1933.

Acocks Green Infants School, Westley Road, 1933

ACOCKS GREEN INFANTS 1933.

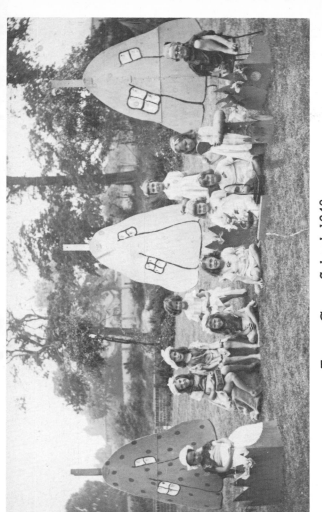

Turves Green School, 1948.

Sunny smiles reflect the weather at St Benedict's Road Junior School, Small Heath, 1956.

PRIESTLEY'S for PIANOS

St Benedict's Road Infants School, Small Heath, 1931.

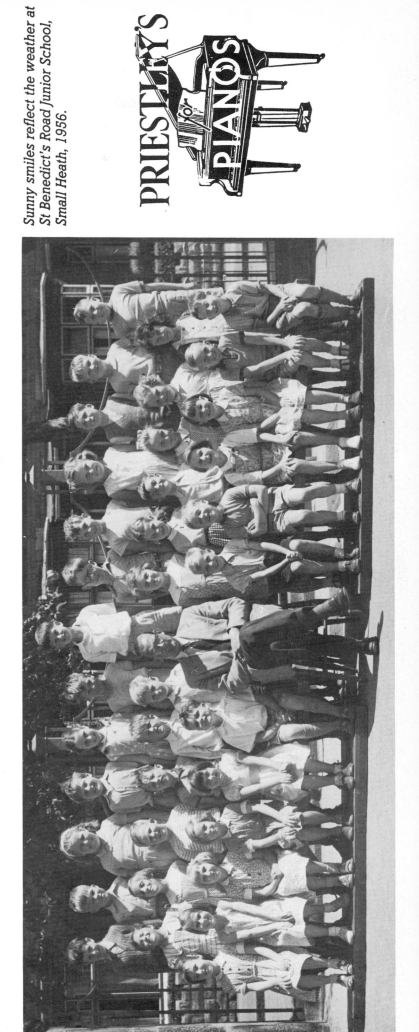

Staff of Foundry Road School, Winson Green, 1959.

South Yardley Methodist Church Boy
Scouts and Wolf Cubs, 1931.

74th Birmingham, 1st Kings Norton Girl
Guides, 1921.

Birmingham Battalion, Boys' Brigade
Annual Display at Alexander Sports
Ground, Perry Barr, 11th June 1938.

THEY ALSO SERVE

The early Fire Brigades belonged to the insurance companies and only those premises bearing the appropriate company's fire-plate (identification mark) would be served in the event of a fire. Birmingham's Fire Brigade came into being in 1873 when the insurance companies handed over all their equipment to the town. This comprised 5 engines, 16 hoses and 13 uniforms -total value £1,000!

We must go back a long way to find the beginnings of a constabulary in Birmingham, to 1716 in fact, when the wording of a petition declared the town of Birmingham as being "governed by a constable". This was not strictly true for there were TWO constables and a headborough (an assistant), who became the prison-keeper with six "thief takers" to help him. An Act of 1773 allowed the appointment of night-watchmen and night constables, but, with no funds available, by 1801 there was still no public watch. Much changed with the Birmingham Police Act (1839) when the force rose to over 300 with principal stations at Beardsworth's Repository, Bath Row, Deritend, Sandpits and Staniforth Street. The turnover in staff was large but the total strength never exceeded 400. Further stations appeared in New Street and Duke Street in 1842, and a matron for the central lock-up was appointed in 1895. (Only two policewomen were on the strength in 1917, this number rising to 30 by 1950.) A new central station for Steelhouse Lane came in 1933 and four years later the total force numbered 1,887 officers of all ranks, comprising 5 Divisions and 24 Sub-divisions all operating from 35 stations. Just after the War ended in 1945, the establishment was raised to 2,000 but with recruiting difficulties mainly due to housing shortages, the actual force remained below this number.

Selly Oak Hospital in Raddlebarn Road was originally the Kings Norton Union Workhouse (1872), and cost £20,000 at that time. Those buildings comprise the present School of Nursing. Land adjoining was purchased and a new Infirmary opened in 1897. The workhouse was housing so many inmates by 1907 that more expansion became necessary. By the mid-1930's specialist laboratories and departments grew into the present extensive hospital complex. In context here, it is fascinating to note that, considering the enormous interest in alternative medicine today, a building demolished in the Old Square in 1890 was in fact a Homeopathic Hospital. The Children's Hospital, Ladywood Road, was opened by King George V and Queen Mary on 21st May 1919. Just nineteen years later, on 14th July 1938, the Queen Elizabeth Hospital was opened by the then Duke of Gloucester, deputising for King George VI and his Queen, Elizabeth (the present Queen Mother), who were unable to attend due to illness. However, in March 1939, the Queen returned to carry out the naming ceremony. A scrapbook of the hospital reveals that on 6th October 1939, vandals attacked 170 of the nurses' bicycles, leaving only 30 unharmed.

Eleven of the first thirteen firemen employed when the Birmingham Fire Brigade was formed, 1874.

The first motor vehicle bought by Birmingham Fire Brigade was this Wolseley Hose Carrier, 1906.

Moseley Fire Brigade, c. 1902.

2nd City Battalion, The Royal Warwickshire Regiment, en route for Yorkshire, July 1915.

6th Battalion, The Royal Warwickshire Regiment, march across Hill Street, 4th August 1914, (the day that Britain declared war on Germany).

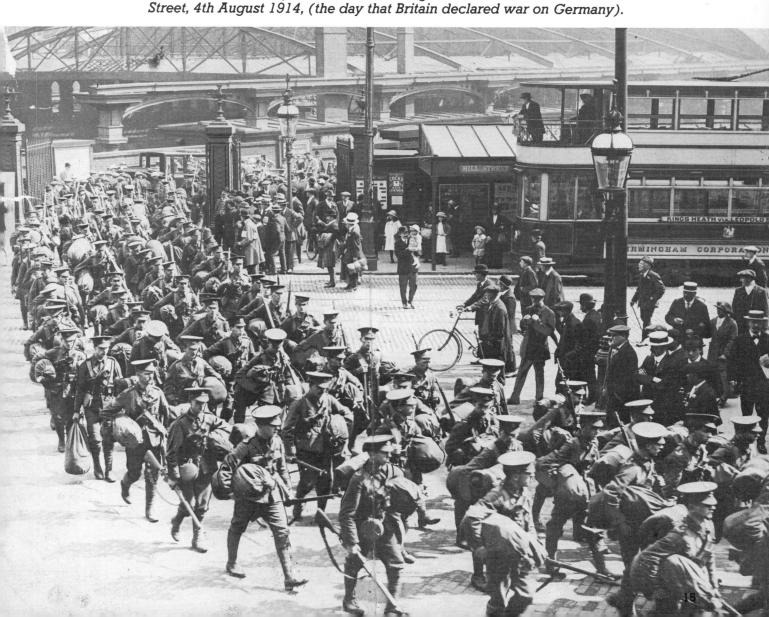

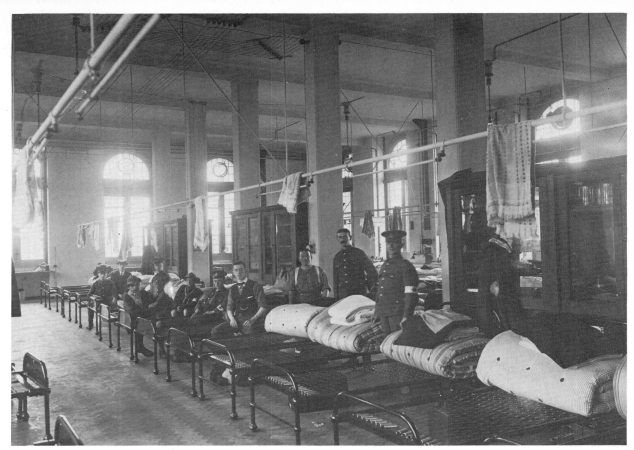

The Military took over the Birmingham University buildings as the First Southern General Hospital. By the end of the war over 67,000 patients had been treated. Bournbrook, 1914.

Royal Orthopaedic Hospital (Newhall St Birmingham)
Medical Officers, Secretary and Nurses, 1897.

Nurses reunion, Selly Oak Hospital, July 1953.

West Heath Hospital Staff, 1954.

British Red Cross Society, Highfield Road, Edgbaston, 1943

FRED GILBERT,
Chief Superintendent.

BIRMINGHAM CORPS.

72, CAMBRIDGE STREET,
THE CRESCENT,
BIRMINGHAM,

March 6th 190 7

Salvation Army Songster Brigade, Jenkins
Street, Small Heath, 1940

To Patients removal from Pershore Road
to Park Hill, Moseley.

Hire of Horse Ambulance	10 . 6
" " Invalid's Carrying Chair & carriage of same	5 . 0
Men's Expenses.	2 . 6
	18 : 0

6th April 1907
Received by cheque
F. Gilbert.
with thanks.

St John Ambulance Brigade, Birmingham
District and Corps. Staff, December 1926.

British Red Cross Society Cadets Band,
Harborne, c. 1956.

Some of the 130 Panda cars of Birmingham City Police Force, Edgbaston, July 1967.

Council Chambers, c. 1935.

THE CITY CENTRE

The city centre has changed but there is still much remaining which is familiar and cherished. From the top of the Bull Ring runs the straight line of New Street all the way to Victoria Square with its statue of Queen Victoria. There also stand the magnificent Council House with its fine porch, and the impressive Town Hall, an absolute masterpiece. This latter building was started in 1832, using Anglesey marble, carried all the way over by canal. Bricks were made on the site from clay turned up by the foundation trenches. It is said to be an imitation and a scaled-down version of the Temple of Castor and Pollux in Rome.

In the old days, walking up New Street, one would once have noticed the lovely, old Gothic building of King Edward VI High School.

Scotcher's in Corporation Street is a shop remembered for its large windows. Pianos and other musical instruments were sold there, and within, there were sound-proofed studios, each with its own piano, for hiring.

Anyone alighting from a tram, perhaps a 21 or 18, in Station Street, might have been swept along by the crowd up the wide steps of New Street Station and across the long, covered bridge. Oh, the smell of the smoke and the steam! Out then into Stephenson Place with its Queen's Hotel, rows of telephone boxes and, of course, the hot-chestnut man.

By 1958, the City Council had decided that the old Market Hall should be demolished, but it was not until early January 1964 that Alderman D.S. Thomas (Chairman) and his Public Works Committee went along to see the first sections of masonry removed. Prior to this, on 13th November 1963, the stallholders packed up their wares to open in the new Bull Ring Centre the next day.

The Bull Ring itself will never be the same again. Markets have been held there for over 800 years and once it had hawkers with their handcarts, orators on their soap-boxes, cheap-jack stalls and palmists. The escapologists were always a draw for the crowds. Yet today, there is, as ever, St Martin's, in the Bull Ring, a very lovely church.

Just off Broad Street, near the new Repertory Theatre, stood Bingley Hall. In 1756 it was Bingley House, the home of the Farmer family, whose daughter married Mr Lloyd, the banker from Edgbaston. By 1849 it was THE show place for trade and industry, but it was demolished by rail developers cutting the New Street tunnel. The new Hall was leased to the Agricultural Exhibition Society from the City for annual shows, including the famous "Ideal Homes Exhibition". How the patrons longed to own the house or bungalow specially built in the Hall for exhibition! Do you remember the new-fangled potato peelers, knife sharpeners and other gadgets touted by the stallholders? Did you, like so many others, search diligently for the lucky stars symbols concealed under the furniture on show? Who could resist hanging on until the last possible moment to see the dazzling, musical water-fountains before dashing off for home on bus or train! A recent fire destroyed the Hall.

No longer can we take tea and eat cakes at Pattison's, Kunzles or The Kardomah, or enjoy a milk-shake at a choice of milk bars. However, shiny, new cafes have come along where good service can still be obtained.

After mourning the passing of so many valued buildings it is encouraging to see that a new responsibility seems to be emerging. Just contemplating the excellent restoration work performed on the Great Western Arcade in 1984, for example, gives one hope for the future.

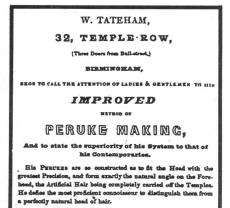

Strike-bound travellers, Snow Hill Station, May 1955.

The imposing facade of Snow Hill Station after closure in 1967.

The Birmingham Post and Mail buildings seem to grow before your eyes, May Day 1951.

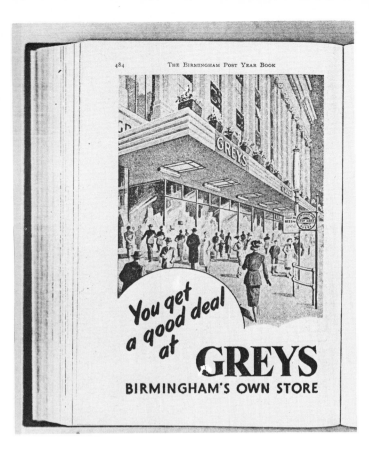

Steelhouse Lane, from Slaney Street, with Weaman Street on the left, 1946. Looking towards the General Hospital.

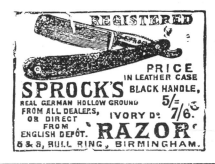

STORES OF OXYGEN.

PROFESSIONAL divers, who remain
under water from two to five minutes
at a time, before submerging themselves take deep inspirations for
about ten minutes. The object is
said to be to store up oxygen, not in
the lung cells, but in the blood-
corpuscles. This renders a temporary
suspension of the breathing possible
by supplying the corpuscles with an
extra quantity of oxygen.

23

The Minories (between Lewis's), November 1938.
This is something of a curio because, due to road work in Bull Street, the traffic was going the wrong way.

The Old Square, with Corporation Street facing, April 1955.

Looking from the Old Square along Corporation Street towards Bull Street, September 1962.

From just below Bull Street we look along Corporation Street in the direction of New Street, 1885.

Corporation Street, 1931, taken from almost the same spot.

1956

GENERAL LITERATURE
CURRENT FICTION
JUVENILES·

MEDICAL,
TECHNICAL and
SCHOOL BOOKS

CHOICE BOOKS
RARE, LIMITED and
SIGNED EDITIONS

BOOK TOKENS
sold and exchanged

Agents by Appointment

for the sale of

Ordnance Survey Maps and Large Scale Plans

CORNISH BROTHERS
LTD.
39, NEW STREET - BIRMINGHAM 2
Telephone Number: MIDland 0569

Stephenson Place, December 1964.
The Queen's Hotel closed two years
later after 112 years.

New Street, taken from the bottom of Bennett's Hill, looking towards Lower Temple Street, 1909.

28

Christchurch Passage and down the steps from Waterloo Street to New Street, October 1969.

New Street with the new overhead lighting system, October, 1934.

29

1936

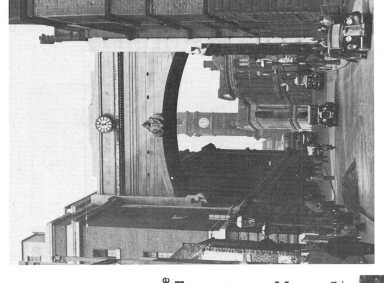

A double opportunity to check your watch! Hill Street, November 1935.

Edmund Street, July 1939.

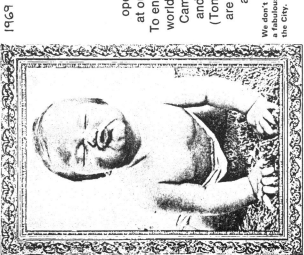

Easy Row, c. 1937.

Paradise Street, February 1959.

Easy Row/Edmund Street, 1912. This is now the site of the Central Library.

Easy Row and Broad Street, July 1946.

Smallbrook Street, June 1956. The Scala disappeared almost exactly 4 years later.

This excellent panoramic view shows many projects under construction near the Inner Ring Road. On the left, the hole in the ground is part of the New Street to Bristol railway line. In the background is the ATV Studio and Exhibition Hall and in the right foreground is the Suffolk Street end of the Great Charles Street tunnel, April 1971.

Queen's Drive, New Street Station, with Hill Street in the distance, April 1958.

High Street, looking towards Dale End, May 1932.

High Street/Moor Street, August 1955.

The Rotunda rises, July 1963.

Pupils of the Blue Coat School arrive at St Martin's, in the Bull Ring, to make a Midland Regional radio broadcast, August 1935. The St Martin's Hotel is in the background.

Christmas shoppers, 1957.

Christmas shoppers, 1937.

 A February afternoon, viewed from the Times building, in 1959.

The "new" Rag Market in Edgbaston Street, August 1957.

OUT & ABOUT

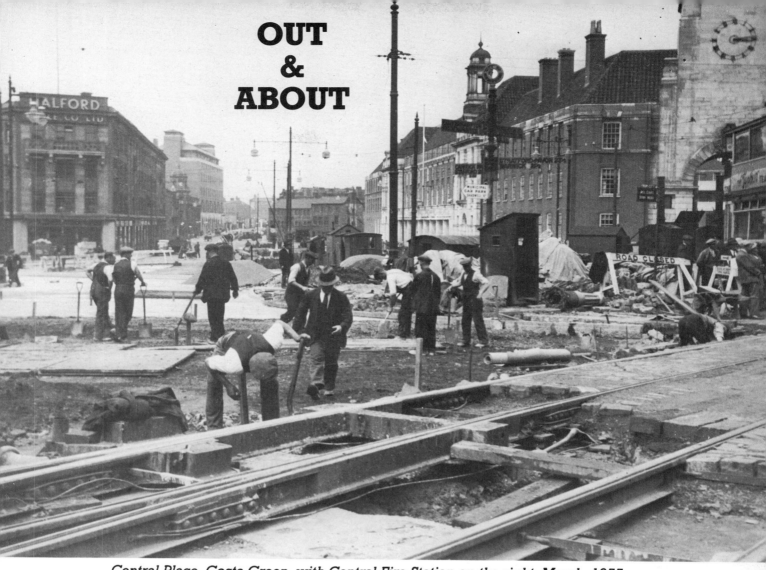

Central Place, Gosta Green, with Central Fire Station on the right, March 1955.

Aston Cross, with Tower Road on the left, April 1952.

High Park Corner/Nechells Park Road, 18th August 1959. Charlie Bottrill remembers the exact date because he bought the camera, his first, from the chemist's, went straight outside and took this photograph of the shop!

Rupert Street, Aston, taken from near Avenue Road, and looking towards Great Lister Street, June 1955.

Lichfield Road, Aston, facing away from the city, with Cuckoo Road halfway down on the right, October 1930.

Summer Lane, Newtown, going from the city centre, c. 1949.

Spring Hill canal bridge, travelling towards Dudley Road, October 1932.

A courtyard in Unett Street, Newtown, 1960.

Darwin Street, Highgate, 1965.

Chapel Terrace, Saltley Road, 1905.

Six Ways, Erdington, from the top of Gravelly Hill North, July 1935.

Salford Bridge, looking towards Gravelly Hill, 1924. The present bridge was opened on 13th October 1926.

Island Road, with a van turning out of Handsworth Dairies (now Birmingham Dairies) on the right, September 1933.

The junction of Birchfield Road and Aston Lane, near the Crown and Cushion, Perry Barr, August 1939. Note the poster of George Easton, famous racing driver - who only used Castrol!

Ladywood Road seen from the Children's Hospital, 1938.

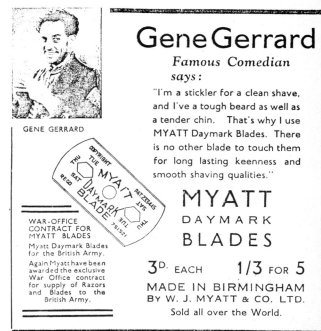
The Reading Room, Balsall Heath Library, 1910.

45

Five Ways, Edgbaston, with Hagley Road on the right, 1958.

Members of the Lee Strathy and Lyall Grant families in Vivian Road, Harborne, 1889. This photograph is of particular interest because the little girl second left became Lady Mayoress in 1940 and her son, Denis Martineau, was made Lord Mayor in 1986.

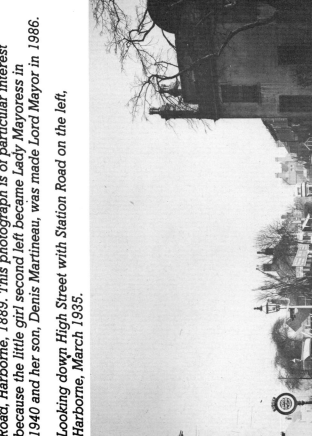

Looking down High Street with Station Road on the right, Harborne, March 1935.

Opposite The Green Man, High Street, Harborne, 1941.

Looking towards Lightwoods Park from the Kings Head corner, Hagley Road, June, 1930.

Jiggins Lane, Bartley Green, from Genners Lane, April 1937.

Quinton Hall, College Road, 1937 (in use as a men's home). It was originally Bourne College.

A view of Quinton from the roof of the Odeon, Warley, with the Clent Hills forming a hazy backdrop, April 1961.

Harborne Lane canal bridge, Selly Oak, with Gibbons Road on the left, July 1931.

50

*Masshouse Lane and Redditch Road viewed from Pershore Road South,
with Kings Norton Green on the right, 1950.*

A village within a city. Moseley, from the top of the Baptist Church in Oxford Road, with a splendid view of Moseley Parish Church, June 1960.

Highfield Road, Yardley Wood, from the Hall Green side, January 1937.

Acocks Green Village, from Shirley Road, 1932.

BIRMINGHAM STAGE-COACH,

In Two *Days* and a half; begins *May* the 24th, 1731.

SET out from the *Swan-Inn* in *Birmingham*, every *Monday* at six a Clock in the Morning, through *Warwick*, *Banbury* and *Alesbury*, to the *Red Lion Inn* in *Aldersgate street*, *London*, every *Wednesday* Morning: And returns from the said *Red Lion Inn* every *Thursday* Morning at five a Clock the same Way to the *Swan-Inn* in *Birmingham* every *Saturday*, at 21 Shillings each Passenger, and 18 Shillings from *Warwick*, who has liberty to carry 14 Pounds in Weight, and all above to pay *One Penny a Pound*.

Perform'd (if God permit)

By Nicholas Rothwell.

The Weekly Waggon sets out every *Tuesday* from the *Nagg's-Head* in *Birmingham*, to the Red Lion Inn aforesaid, every *Saturday*; and returns from the said Inn every *Monday*, to the *Nagg's-Head* in *Birmingham* every *Thursday*.

Note. By the said Nicholas Rothwell at Warwick, all Persons may be furnished with a By-Coach, Chariot, Chaise, or Hearse, with a Mourning Coach and able Horses, to any Part of Great Britain, at reasonable Rates: And also Saddle Horses to be had.

The Swan Inn, Coventry Road, Yardley, c. 1895.

Wagon Lane/Coventry Road, Yardley, February 1937.

LEA TAVERN, LEA HALL.

*Lea Tavern, Lea Village,
1937.*

*Coventry Road, Hay Mills,
with Kings Road on the
immediate left, 1925.*

*The Fox & Goose from
Stechford Lane, Washwood
Heath, March 1932.*

Bordesley Green looking across towards Blake Lane, October 1928.

Bordesley Green East, September 1932. Corner of the former Ritz Cinema on the far right.

Belchers Lane, Alum Rock, from Caldwell Road, towards Cotterills Lane, February 1925.

Alum Rock Road, March 1931.

EVENTS

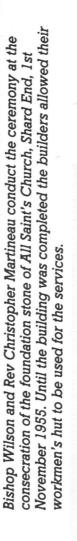

Bishop Wilson and Rev Christopher Martineau conduct the ceremony at the consecration of the foundation stone of All Saint's Church, Shard End, 1st November 1955. Until the building was completed the builders allowed their workmen's hut to be used for the services.

Edward, Prince of Wales, formally opens the Birmingham end of the Wolverhampton/Birmingham Road, 2nd November 1927

Opening of the General Hospital by Princess Christian, accompanied by Princess Victoria, 7th July 1897.

Opening of the Hall of Memory, Broad Street, by Prince Arthur of Connaught, 4th July 1925.

*King George VI and Queen Elizabeth (now the Queen Mother)
leave the Accident Hospital after their visit to the city on 7th
November 1945.*

The Queen meets Wilfred Martineau at the opening of the Colleges of Technology, Commerce and Art, Gosta Green, 1955.

Wolf Cubs from all over Birmingham attend the 40th anniversary Thanksgiving Service in the Central Hall, Corporation Street, 24th June 1956.

Palm Sunday at the Parish Church of St Andrew, Oxhill Road, Handsworth, 1921.

Guides and Brownies from Handsworth and Aston enjoy a Spring trip to the Lickey Hills, April 1954.

Firemen and public alike relax at the annual Fire Brigade Display at Calthorpe Park, 1932.

The annual outing of the Lozells Picture House staff (including the musicians of the eight piece orchestra) Lozells Road, 1926.

A Sunday School outing from Greet Methodist Chapel, c. 1900.

"Children of the Poor" taken on a summer outing to Sutton Park, organised by the Birmingham Cinderella Club, 1908.

An outing from Kings Norton Green in 1900. Only the ground floor of the building remains today (as a Chinese take-away).

Bertram Mills Circus parade along Coventry Road, Hay Mills, 1951.

The Onion Fair at the Serpentine Fairground, Aston, October 1960.
The annual event finished in 1969 after more than 550 years.

*VE celebrations in Hassop Road, Great Barr,
May 1945.*

*Coronation party in Anderton Street,
Ladywood, 1937.*

*Nursery rhymes were the theme at
Cranbourne Road Junior School Parents' Day,
Kingstanding, 1934.*

The famous broadcaster Kenneth Horne (with buttonhole - and hair!) sits in the centre of this group from the Triplex Safety Glass Co. Ltd. The occasion is the Annual Christmas Dance at the West End Ballroom, c. 1928. He rose to the position of Sales Director with the Kings Norton firm and also, at one time, owned a record shop in Pershore Road, Cotteridge.

65

Sir Oswald Mosley at a private conference of the British Union of Fascists in Stafford Street, 7th October 1937, to discuss progress and future activity.

A moment of drama as the old Stechford Station burns, May 1956.

The last tram leaves Miller Street depot, Newtown, 6th July 1953.

The end of an era as the city's last gas lamp is removed from Duke Street, Gosta Green, 3rd January 1975. In the 1930's Birmingham had 35,000 gas lamps and as late as 1967 11,000 remained.

The first passenger train since November 1934 at Harborne Station, 3rd June 1950.

ON THE MOVE

Before the age of the motor car, what fun it was to take an open-top char-a-banc or a Midland Red bus out to the Lickey Hills, Sutton Park or Stratford-upon-Avon! When warmer days came the bus conductors started wearing caps somewhat lighter than the ones they wore during winter and then we knew that summer had arrived. In our excitement we never seemed to mind the hard seats and the draughty windows. Prior to that the first tram-line was opened for public traffic in Birmingham in 1873 and by 1890 trams were battery-powered down the Bristol Road. Perhaps the most complicated points system was on the City to Erdington route at Salford Bridge (near the present Spaghetti motorway junction).

Lifford Canal Wharf, looking towards Breedon Bridge, Pershore Road, Stirchley, c. 1904.

THE FIRST MOTOR CYCLE IN HANDSWORTH WOOD, 1902   *Photo : Philip Whitehouse*
Built by Milbrowe Smith, Engineer, Handsworth. 1½ h.p. Minerva Engine, Surface Carburetter, Wet Battery, Trembler Ignition, Hand Oil Pump, Rawhide Belt. Eadie Fittings throughout. Sturmey Archer B.P. Brake. Front Band Brake. 2in. Palmer Tyres, Brooks Saddle. Weight 120 lbs.
A Founder Member, B'ham M.C. Club, 26/3/03. Member Assoc. Pioneer Motor Cyclists, 1903

Stratford Road, Sparkbrook, c. 1912.

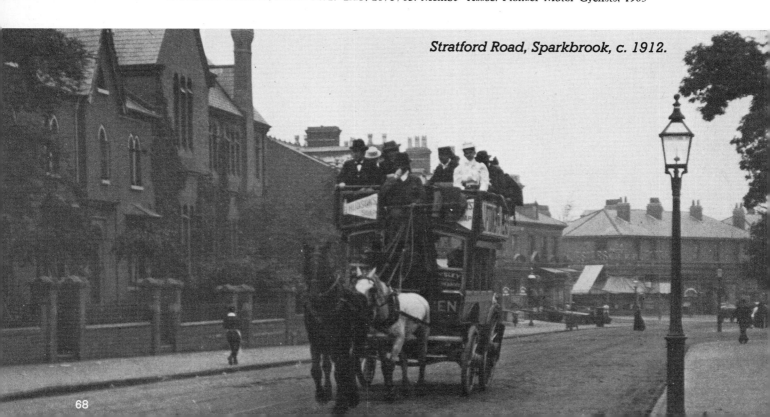

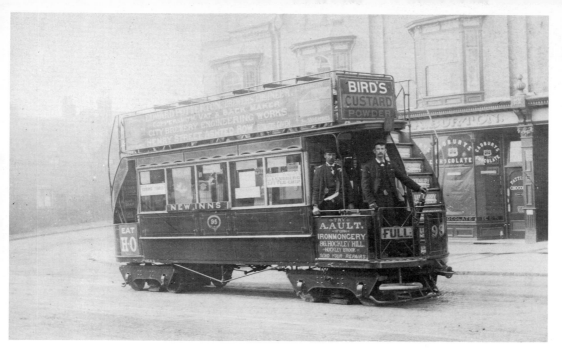

Cable tram at New Inns, Holyhead Road, Handsworth, c. 1900.

Electric battery tram, Suffolk Street, c. 1900.

Steam tram, Stratford Road/Farm Road, Sparkbrook, 1905.

 First electric tram in Handsworth. Soho Road, July 1911.

 Digbeth, June 1949. The Institute is now the Civic Hall.

The Tilling-Stevens solid-tyred "Knifeboard" bus, 1922.

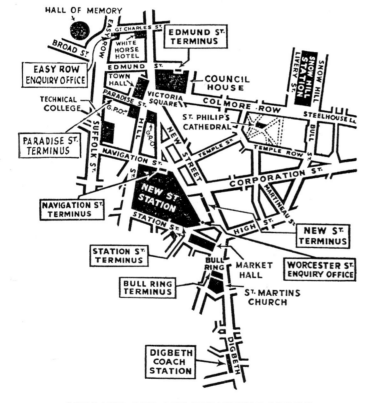

MIDLAND RED BUS DEPARTURE POINTS

New Midland Red buses, Carlyle Works, Edgbaston, April 1955.

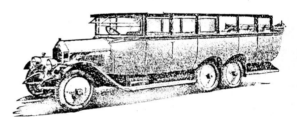

Fifty Jowett four-seaters were purchased by the Metropolitan Police from Hydes of John Bright Street in 1927.

MOTORING PLEASANT and MOTORISTS POPULAR.

DO carry your driving licence.
DO keep to the left of the road.
DO go slow past schools and in populous places.
DO overtake on the right, after seeing that the road in front is clear.
DO give warnings with the right arm when slowing down or turning to the off-side.
DO, other things being equal, watch for and give way to traffic approaching from the right.
DO pass a led horse on its near side.
DO conform to the lighting and registration regulations.
DO recognize warning signs and speed restriction notices.
DO realize the discomfort to others of dust and mud splashing.

Islington Row, November 1939.

Licence No. 14898   ~~920~~   Motor Car Act, 1903.

CITY OF BIRMINGHAM.

RENEWAL of LICENCE to DRIVE a MOTOR CAR or CYCLE.

George Wyton
of *120 Manchester Street B'ham*
is hereby licensed to drive a MOTOR CAR or CYCLE for the period of Twelve
Months from the _____ 8th _____ day of _____ March 1915
until the _____ day of _____ March 1916 inclusive.

E. O. Hiley Town Clerk

Date of issue _____ 9/3/15

N.B.—Particulars of any endorsement of any Licence previously held by the person licensed must be entered on the back of this Licence.

Fee, 5/-

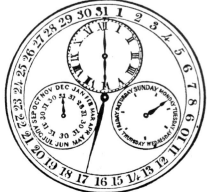

IMPORTANT TO
BANKERS, MERCHANTS, RAILWAY COMPANIES,
AND THE PUBLIC GENERALLY.

NOW EXHIBITING, at the EXPOSITION.

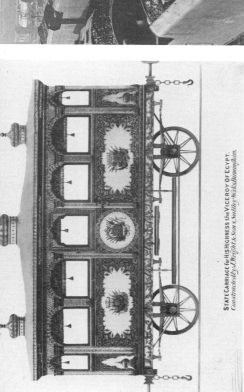

Monument Lane Station, Railway Wharf, St Vincent Street, Edgbaston, October 1958, shortly before closure.

Saltley sidings, October 1962.

Whit Monday holidaymakers wait at New Street Station for the early morning train to Rhyl, 2nd May 1961.

STATE CARRIAGE for HIS HIGHNESS the VICEROY OF EGYPT,
Constructed by J. Wright & Son's, Saltley Works Birmingham.

AT WORK

It has been said of Birmingham that its artisans and tradesmen could produce anything from a pin to a steam-roller. By updating, we can probably broaden this to anything from a microchip to a motor-car.

So involved was Birmingham with the industrial life of Britain that in 1920, at Castle Bromwich, the first British Industries Fair (B.I.F.) was staged. The world went there to see the quality and might of British manufacturing. The site now forms part of the Castle Vale housing estate.

Hard work is thirsty work. Not surprisingly, beers, ales and stouts became prime local products, famed throughout the land. The maltster, John Ansell, began trading in 1857 and, with family help, he had a thriving business in Moseley. By the turn of the century his licensed premises had risen in number from 96 to 388. Outgrowing its premises, the brewery moved to Aston in 1934. Davenports, famous for their "Beer at Home" service, began in Bath Row in 1830. Henry Mitchell and William Butler, before forming their partnership, were successful brewers in their own right. By 1900 Mitchells and Butlers Cape Hill site had grown to over 60 acres and employed 1,000 people.

John Boyd Dunlop, a Belfast vet, patented a pneumatic tyre in 1888 and produced his first samples in Aston before moving to Fort Dunlop, Erdington in 1917.

Heaton's, forerunners of the Birmingham Mint, in their early days had supplied coins to the Royal Mint. Coins marked "H" for Heaton's and "KN" for Kings Norton are now rare.

Described as the city of 1,001 trades, here are a few examples of Birmingham products:
armaments, arc lighting and lighthouse apparatus, bedsteads, buttons, brewing, cocoa and chocolate, cycles, coins and medals, fish hooks, hollow-ware, jewellery, locks and bolts, motor vehicles, nails, needles and pins, parasols, pewter, refrigerators, ropes, rubber, sauce and vinegar, salt, swords, tools, tinplate - and even magic lantern slides!

Great Hampton Street, 1901.

*Marks and Spencer's shop 42a, High Street in 1904. (Original premises were at Snow Hill from 1898).
The premises were considerably extended between 1933 and 1939 only to be destroyed in the air-raid of 9th
April 1941. Temporary premises opened in 1946 using former YMCA huts. Rebuilding of the present store
began in 1951 on the same site.*

Vivian Road, Harborne, c. 1904.

Christmas 1930. The Hughes family have had a shop at 1464 Pershore Road, Stirchley, since 1899. Albert, seen on the right, is still active today.

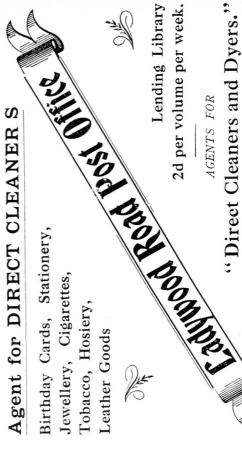

1049 and 1051 Coventry Road, Hay Mills, c. 1908.

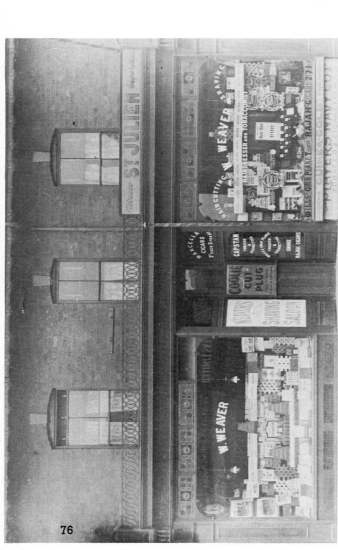

Lashford's butcher's shop, High Street/Poplar Road, Kings Heath, c. 1916.

76

New Job Every Minute for a Year! 1937

Once every minute during the last twelve months one person got a job.   That was part of the evidence of
Britain's revived prosperity quoted yesterday by Mr. Walter Elliot, Minister for Agriculture, when he spoke
at Glasgow.   Every minute of the year—day and night—a job was offered and snapped up.   Every minute
one more person went out with renewed hope to earn wages.   And at the end of the year the wages were
still being earned—hundreds of thousands of new jobs were still in existence.   Still further prosperity is assured
by widespread Coronation contracts on a big scale.   One London hotel announced yesterday that it is to
spend £65,000 on redecorating and refurnishing suites for Coronation Year.

Bill Warmsley's cafe, St Johns Road/Dolphin Road, Sparkhill, 1952.

These premises in Ledsam Street, Ladywood, 1965, were once the scene of a crime which shocked the whole country. In April 1883 armed detectives raided the shop and found that behind the innocent front, as a paint and wallpaper dealer, Alfred Whitehead had made enough explosives in his small back kitchen to blast a large area and kill hundreds of people.

Lichfield Road, Aston, August 1956.

A supply of paraffin, at 1 penny a pint, is ready leave Carpenters Road, Lozells, 1905.

George Bailey outside Mr Harding's house, near the bakery in Coventry Road, Yardley, c. 1925.

Stockfield Road, South Yardley, 1928.

Farm hands and workers from the asphalt yard enjoy the midday air outside the Hare & Hounds, Holly Lane, Kingstanding, 1919.

A stout that gives you a new lease of life —and it's not bitter!

Most stout has a slightly bitter taste, which many people like. But Mackeson's is rather smoother and softer — and some greatly prefer it. They find fresh strength and life in every glass, when the long day's work is over at last.

That's why some people prefer

MACKESON'S

BREWED AND BOTTLED BY WHITBREAD

DEPOT: KING EDWARD'S PLACE, BIRMINGHAM, 1

The Woodman, Easy Row. Surprisingly the photograph was taken as recently as 1964.

The new bottling plant in operation at Ansell's brewery, Aston, September 1937.

Cadbury employees at Bournville Cafe, Leahouse Road, c. 1913.

Cadbury girls at breakfast on the terrace, September 1933.

FAR TOO FREE TRADING.   1901

SUGAR: "There are those Foreign Manufacturers coming in free to compete with English-made
goods, and we bear the brunt."
COAL: "I shall strike."
INCOME TAX: "Alas! I can only groan."

Smithfield Market from Bradford Street, c. 1932.

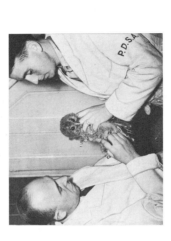

Mr Le Cren (left) and his assistant examine "Owlbert" the owl, June 1939.

Market Hall, 1901. Fish and game stalls (left) and dining stalls opposite.

Early morning in Smithfield Market, April 1936.

82

Export Bay, BSA Works, Golden Hillock Road, Small Heath, August 1948.

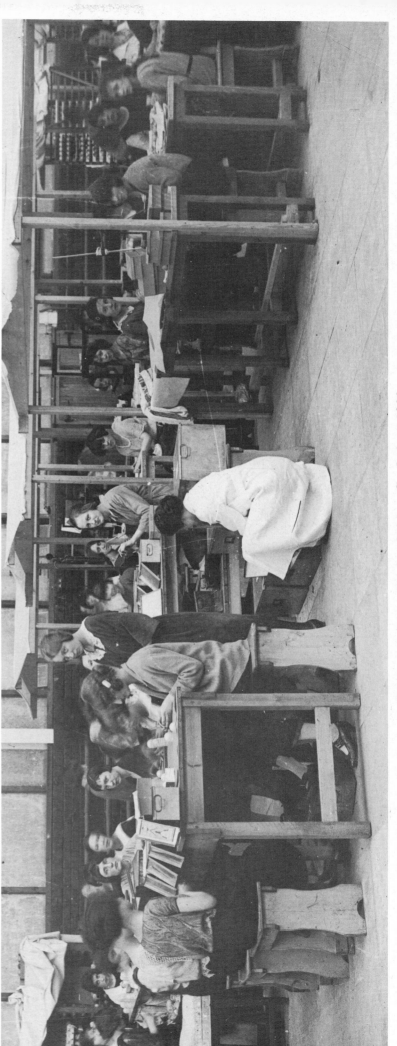

Tennis Ball Dept., Dunlop Rubber Co. Ltd., c. 1928

Workers at Nock's Brickworks, Erdington, 1890

Rover Works, Kings Road,
Tyseley, 1917.

Arthur Gossage Ltd., Ward Street, Aston, 1928.
Manufacturing packing cases the firm, established
1780, is led today by Colin Gossage and is
based in Bishop Street.

The Birmingham Mint Ltd., Icknield Street, Hockley, 1938.

Southalls, Alum Rock Road, 1927. 450 girls were employed in the workshop.

The original Austin factory building in 1906.

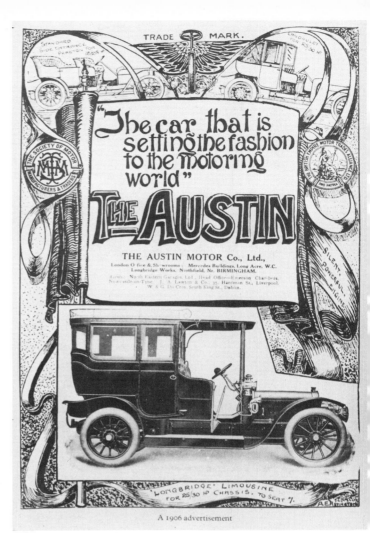

A 1906 advertisement

Fitting shop (south side) Austin
Works, 1923.

The final polish given to cars coming
off the production line at the Austin
Motor Co. Ltd., 1936. The brillant
lights enable the polishers to detect
and rectify any slight flaws.

Notice to the Printing Trade

(OFFICIAL).

Extract from Birmingham Post, May 6th. 1926

When the present general strike is ended His Majesty's Government will take effectual measures to prevent the victimization by trades unions of any man who remains at work, or who may return to work, and no settlement will be agreed to by His Majesty's Government which does not provide for this for a lasting period and for its enforcement if necessary by penalties. No man who does his duty loyally to the country in the present crisis will be left unprotected by the State from subsequent reprisals.

Old Court House, High Street, 1900.

1929.

Birmingham Post Reporting Staff, 1901.

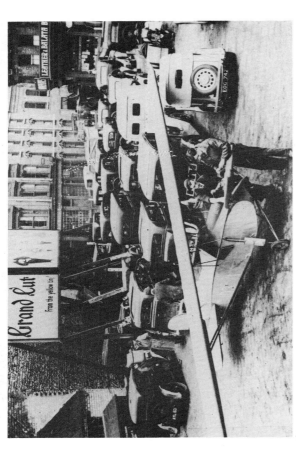

The latest battery equipment at Central Telephone Exchange, Newhall Street, March 1938. ⇩

⇦ *An unusual item for sale on a second-hand car lot opposite Milk Street, Digbeth, 1951. "Wagtail", built by F.W. Taylor and L. Bracey, fetched £25.*

⇨ *GPO Engineering Section, Fordrough Lane, Bordesley Green, c. 1945.*

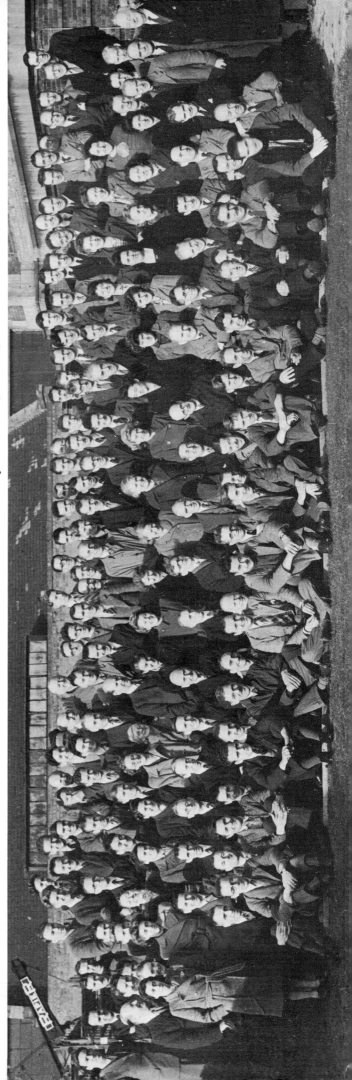

AT PLAY

In the past theatres were very popular in Birmingham. Cinemas were in abundance and the suburbs had their fair share. These attracted huge audiences yet the pleasure of cinema-going was enchanced by a trip to the city centre to see the latest films.

The City of Birmingham Symphony Orchestra began life on 5th September 1920 as the City of Birmingham Orchestra, operating first from the Theatre Royal before basing itself at the Town Hall. A noted and well-respected conductor in the 1950's was George Weldon, who had as his leader the equally well-known Norris Stanley.

Horse Racing began in Four Oaks Park in 1881 and continued there until 1892. The Earl of Bradford's estate, Bromford Bridge, became Birmingham's Race Course in 1884 but has now disappeared. The site is now the Tame Valley housing estate, many of its roads bearing names associated with other race courses.

Warwickshire County Cricket Club, formed in 1882, won its first County Championship in 1911 and gained others in 1951 and 1972. The Gillette Cup was won in 1966 and 1968. The lovely Egbaston ground staged its first Test Match in 1902. Among its famous players rank R.E.S (Bob) Wyatt, Tom Dollery, Eric Hollies, M.J.K. Smith and Bob Willis.

Birmingham City F.C. started as Small Heath Alliance in 1875 but dropped the tag "Alliance" thirteen years later. Matches were played on waste ground near Arthur Street until the move to Muntz Street, Small Heath, in 1877. The Club became "Birmingham" in 1905 and moved a year later to its present ground, St Andrew's. The eventual change to "Birmingham City" came in 1945. The Blues won the Football League Cup in 1963, having been runners-up in the European Fair's Cup in 1960 and 1961.

Aston Villa started out as a cricket club in 1872 but in October 1874, four members met in Heathfield Road, Villa Cross and decided to form a football team. Professional status came in 1885 and the club was formed into a Limited Company in 1896. The move to Villa Park took place in 1897. Villa have been Division 1 champions seven times, runners-up eight times, Football League Cup winners three times and winners of the European Cup and European Super Cup in successive years. The famous double achievement of League Champions and F.A. Cup winners came in 1896/97.

In the mid 1930's cycling clubs were extremely popular. The West Midlands Section of the National Clarion Cycling Club, between 1933 and 1936, covered a total mileage of 11,037 (a weekly average of 53 miles). In 1936 their longest run in one day was of 113 miles and the shortest 22 miles.

Moseley Football Club have been playing rugby at their H.Q., The Reddings, for over 100 years.

Rugby stalwarts of Moseley Football Club.

⬆ *Aston Villa F.C., 1895/6.*   ⬇ *Birmingham City F.C., 1914/15.*

Sports & Pastimes Exhibition,

BINGLEY HALL, BIRMINGHAM,

Open Daily from 11 a.m. to 10 p.m.

A BRILLIANT SPECTACLE—

Motors, Cycles, Guns, Gymnastics, Athletics, and Working Exhibits.

Visited by Thousands Daily.

THIS WEEK—BAND OF THE
NORTHUMBERLAND HUSSARS.
(Conductor, Mr. H. G. Amers.)

IMPORTANT.
Owing to the great success of MESSRS.
ADELER AND SUTTON'S PIERROTS, whose
mirth-provoking Entertainment has given such
complete satisfaction, they have been retained to
appear again this week. Every Afternoon at 2-30
and Twice each Evening at 6 and 8 o clock, with
the addition of LAURIE WYLIE and HIS MERRY
MANNIKINS, and SAM CLARE, Baritone.

CHARLIE HARVEY, the Side-splitting Comedian

W. G. SUTTON and EDWIN ADELER, Birmingham's Old Favourites, and

DOUGLAS RANDALL, Solo Pianist.

Open Rifle Competitions for all comers, with
valuable Prizes, Afternoon and Evening.

Ping Pong.—Open Mixed Competition, To-day
(Friday,) October 17th.

BILLIARDS. FISHING, &c.

JAPANESE ART EXHIBITION. Unique and
Costly Collection of Curios; WONDERFUL
WORKING EXHIBITS, by Operators from the
Birmingham Blind Institution; VOLUNTEER
RIFLE SHOOTING COMPETITION: Prizes
value £5; Entrance Fee, 1s., entries to be made to
Mr. C. Dixon, at the Range. TEAM MATCHES,
between Clubs of the Midland Rifle League; Teams
of 10 a side, all to count; 10 shots.

Cotteridge Boys F.C., 1920/21.

*Handsworth New Road School, Winson Green, Senior Boys
1st team, 1920/21.*

Castle Bromwich Aeroplane Factory F.C., 1945

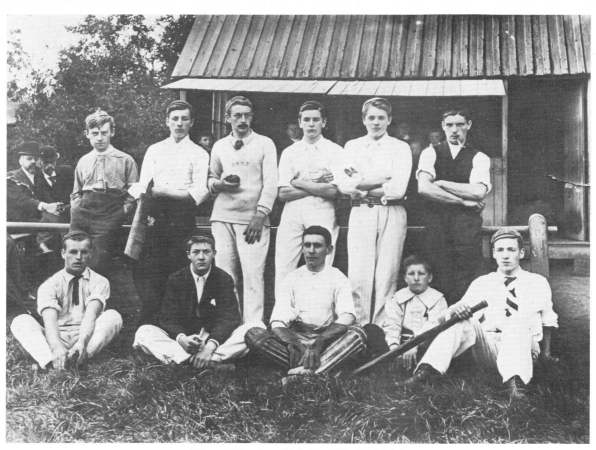

Kings Norton Cricket Club, 1894.

Warwickshire County Cricket Club, 1919.

THE FIRST TEST MATCH.

ENGLAND v. AUSTRALIA.

THE quiet annals of our Edgbaston life have been stirred to its inmost recesses. The struggle between the home team and our Colonial offspring will long be a theme for the cricket world. The play, the weather, and the result have alike been extraordinary.

MUCH INK WILL BE SPILT

and many theories exhausted in the endeavour to account for the remarkable collapse of Australia on the second day. Good bowling, bad batting, good fielding, and a bad light may perhaps sum up the main features of the reason why

A RECORD HAS BEEN ESTABLISHED

on the Edgbaston ground. It was with some difficulty that I managed to secure a seat on Thursday in the Pavilion. The élite of Birmingham had come down early in great force, some enthusiasts, I understand, putting in an appearance as

EARLY AS NINE O'CLOCK.

Many came armed with field glasses, luncheon-baskets, waterproofs, and all the paraphernalia generally noticeable on the race-course. The beautifully dressed ladies had carefully donned

THEIR LARGEST MATINEE HATS,

much to the discomfort of those who sat behind them—for the seats in the Pavilion in front are not raised, and those in the third and fourth row have no chance of viewing the game when the field of vision is completely obscured by these enormous head gear, so much out of place on an occasion of this kind. Many and loud were the complaints uttered around me. Several

VERY NICE PEOPLE

behind lamented that they could see nothing of the game. When will these votaries of fashion have some little consideration for other people? The grievance is an old one, but it never seems to occur to these much adorned ones that they are giving much

MORE PAIN THAN PLEASURE.

The scene on Thursday was a brilliant one. I have never seen so many people on the ground before. The unanimous expression of delight by the massed crowd at a good bit of fielding, or a good stroke by a batsman, was very impressive. Nothing escaped them, and their verdict was frank and decisive.

A DARK CLOUD

hung over the town in the morning. The flags hung motionless against their poles, and the smoke went straight up showing bluey-white against the dark background of the threatening cloud, and then when it looked like tempest the wind sprang up from a new quarter, the cloud

ROLLED AWAY,

the sun appeared once more, and the day remained fine, fortunately for England. If a change had come over the scene, the same might have been said of the game. The most gloomy forecasts were entertained by the supporters of the home team when

FRY WAS CAUGHT

without scoring, and MacLaren was run out after making only nine. But our cup of sorrow seemed full when Ranji was caught by Armstrong. Then was the winter of our discontent

MADE GLORIOUS SUMMER

by the magnificent stand made—just at the right time—by Jackson and Tyldesley. How thankful we were when Jones and Darling

---

THE King's Heath Church Fancy Fair has been doing great business this week. To-morrow (Saturday) is the last day, and there will be plenty of fun in the evening.

I UNDERSTAND that our city will shortly have a new and very attractive café. A company is being formed, and Mr. T. Fletcher, our well-known townsman and Councillor, is to be managing director. The site is one of the finest in the city. The property recently occupied by Norton and Co., with frontages in Corporation Street, Fore Street and Cannon Street, has been acquired, and a most comprehensive scheme proposed by the executive. The new café will be conducted on popular lines, and will, I predict, become one of the favourite resorts for city men.

AFTER a period of excitement during which the mental equilibrium of the city was sadly disturbed, Birmingham has again settled down to its wonted condition. The suburbs were rather loth to part with all their glories of flags and bunting, but even they have relapsed into a peaceful calm, undisturbed save for an occasional dog-fight or runaway motor car. It is certainly a good thing that the town was content with one day's revelling, for had the rejoicings extended longer, many citizens would have needed treatment for deafness. On Monday the pandemonium was terrific, it even penetrated to the calm and unruffled atmosphere of our office, where it caused a feeling of unrest in at least one journalistic cranium.

---

both failed to bring off catches which, if successful, would have once more plunged us into the depths of despair. How

WE SHOUTED

when Tyldesley passed his hundred. Ah! those were moments worth living for. Even when all thought the end was near, Lockwood and Rhodes added run after run.

AUSTRALIA, NOW ROUSED

to the gravity of the situation, bowled and fielded with all the skill at their command, but still our men seemed invincible, do what they could the Colonials failed to separate

THE GALLANT PAIR.

In fact, they never did get them out, for on Friday, with the score at 376, the English captain declared the innings closed, and Lockwood and Rhodes carried out their bats for 52 and 38 respectively. The scene at luncheon time was remarkable. Full advantage was taken of Mr. Heath's admirable catering arrangements, and thousands might have been seen enjoying an al fresco meal on the slopes of the embankment.

WELL FURNISHED BASKETS

were brought out and the contents discussed under novel conditions. I noticed a small army of photographers who had come prepared to take advantage of the occasion, ranging themselves on the field in front of the Pavilion awaiting the appearance of the players. Seats were brought out, and the usual preparations made for

GROUPING THE VICTIMS.

But to the consternation of the operators, and the delight of the public, MacLaren came out and ordered them off the ground. He would not allow the time to be wasted in promoting the interest of the photographic trade. One or two, however,

WISER IN THEIR GENERATION,

came provided with hand cameras, and unobtrusively secured snapshots of the teams as they passed the gate of the enclosure. The sergeant gate-keeper succeeded admirably in keeping the people from passing backwards and forwards when the bowling was at the Pavilion end,

AND STERNLY SUPPRESSED

any infringement of the rules. At tea-time, nevertheless, license was given to the waiters from four o'clock till closing time to tread upon our toes and crush past us laden with trays of

TEA AND CAKES,

much to the annoyance of the cricket-loving public who take the game seriously. It is a pity that some arrangement is not made for the two quite distinctive classes of people—those who come to see the game and those who make a kind of fashionable function or a picnic of the affair. Both are

QUITE WITHIN THEIR RIGHTS,

but their interests clash, and I suggest that they should be kept apart, like the smokers and non-smokers. The heavy rains of Friday night and of the morning of Saturday quite spoilt the chances of

A VICTORY FOR ENGLAND,

and although the sun came out and the afternoon of the last day of play was bright, warm, and fine, alas! the ground was sodden and play impossible until after five. When I arrived on Saturday afternoon about 3-30, I found the Pavilion crowded,

ALL EDGBASTON

seemed to be there. But the deserted appearance of the ground and the empty stands proclaimed an off-day. The hope that some play might yet be witnessed brought the public down in their thousands. The roads outside were

BLACK WITH PEOPLE,

but the doors were closed. About four o'clock it became advisable to open the gates. The Surrey poet (Craig) had interviewed the many-headed outside, and brought back news that they were willing to pay for admission even if there was no play.

MR. JESSE COLLINGS

and other influential persons strongly advised the opening of the gates. This at last was accordingly done, with the result that 15,000 quickly lined, or banked themselves, round the ground. At the town end there was a regrettable occurrence, and many were injured in

THE UGLY RUSH

which took place. A long wait then ensued while the pitch dried. The big and little umpires came out and went back again. The public were very patient, and whiled away the time as best they could. Many frequented

THE HANDSOME TENTS

erected by Messrs. N. Budd and Son, where they found means for quenching their ardour and their thirst. Not to disappoint the people, the captains allowed the game to proceed at 5-15. But

THE GROUND WAS TOO WET,

and the time all too short for anything of importance to be done. At 6-25 stumps were drawn, and the most remarkable game—a game of vicissitudes and surprises, and long to be remembered—came to an end.

E. C. MOUNTFORT.

Sheldon Cycling Club, Three Horse Shoes Inn,
Coventry Road, Sheldon, c. 1900

Joe Sutton plays a tee shot at the short 10th at the opening of the Great Barr Golf Club, 3rd May 1961.
He is still the club's Pro a quarter of a century later.

Bournville Park Bowling Club, 1924.

Moseley Quoit and Bowling Club, 1875.

St Mark's Gymnastics Club, Ladywood 1937.

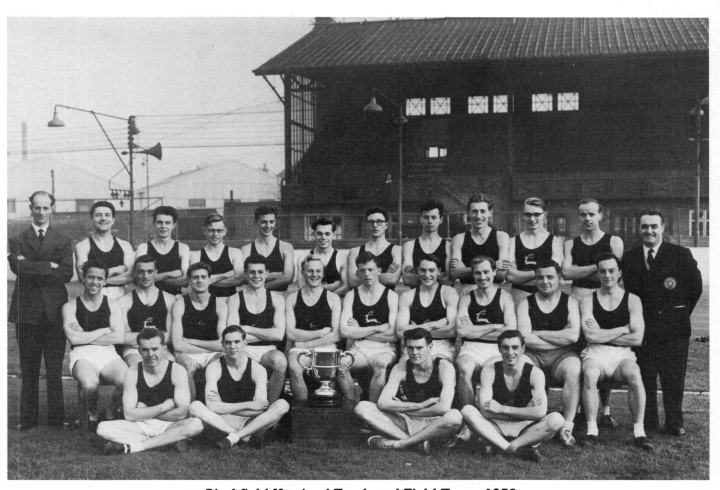

Birchfield Harriers' Track and Field Team, 1956.

FESTIVAL OF BRITAIN IN BIRMINGHAM

JUNE 6 and 7
A FESTIVAL OF BRITAIN'S DANCES
Central Hall, 7 p.m.
Tickets from W. H. Priestley & Son Ltd., 112 New Street

JUNE 7, 8 and 9
FESTIVAL EXHIBITION and OLD FOLKS AT HOME FAIR
Bingley Hall, 11 a.m. - 8.30 p.m.
Saturday (June 9), 1 p.m. - 8.30 p.m.

JUNE 9
VETERAN CAR RALLY
Civic Centre, 10 a.m.

JUNE 9
DISPLAY OF PHYSICAL RECREATION
Villa Park, 2.45 p.m.
Dancing, gymnastics, games, athletics
Band of H.M. Grenadier Guards

Seats: 5s., 3s., 2s. Standing, 1s. 6d. Children 6d.
Tickets from Dale, Forty & Co. Ltd., Alan G. Priestley Ltd. and Lewis's Ltd.

OFFICIAL PROGRAMME PRICE 6d.
from INFORMATION DEPARTMENT, COUNCIL HOUSE
and 57 CORPORATION STREET, BIRMINGHAM
Festival Organiser's Office:
24 EDMUND STREET

BIRMINGHAM HIPPODROME
Telephone—MIDland 2576-77

PROGRAMME

6.40	TWICE NIGHTLY	8.50
MONDAY, APRIL 1939 (GOOD FRIDAY EXCEPTED)		

MMENCING

VARIETY

1 OVERTURE .... Selected

2 SERENO & JUNE TRIO .... Equilibrists

3 ALEC FINLAY .... Mother's Favourite Scottish Comedian

4 ELIMAR .... Novelty Juggler

5 ROSS, PIERRE & SWEENEY .... Three Radio Clowns

6 'FATS' WALLER
The World's Foremost Rhythm Pianist and Master of "Swing"

7 **INTERMISSION**
HIPPODROME ORCHESTRA Under the direction of GEORGE STEELE

8 THE THREE STOOGES With Archie McKay .... Public Enemies 1-2-3

9 JONES & THOMAS .... "The Woman Always Pays"

10 THE MILLS BROTHERS .... Four Boys and a Guitar

11 CECIL LYLE .... "The Magical Milliner"
with Lucille Lafarge & Company
A Fantasy of Fashion and Illusion

SAVAGE SOUTH AFRICA,

FROM EARL'S COURT, LONDON.
Under the Direction of FRANK E. FILLIS and J. PITT HARDACRE.

ASTON LOWER GROUNDS, BIRMINGHAM.

In consequence of enormous success,

One Week longer.
One Week longer.

POSITIVELY CLOSING SATURDAY, JUNE 22nd, 1901

Major Wilson's Last Stand.
THE BATTLE OF ELANDSLAAGTE.

AN EDUCATIONAL EXHIBITION OF SOUTH AFRICAN DAILY LIFE,
With its Great and Varying Crowd of
REAL BOERS,
BRITONS, SOLDIERS, SAILORS, ZULUS, MATABELES, MALAYS,
To extent of
FOUR HUNDRED PERSONS;
HORSES, PONIES, MULES, BULLOCKS, ZEBRAS, WILDEBEESTS, BABOONS, and the
MARVELLOUS ELEPHANTS,
TO THE NUMBER OF 200.

SPECIAL MORNING PERFORMANCES
Every Saturday at 11 a.m.
To which all CHILDREN are admitted for THREEPENCE Each.
AN INTERESTING OBJECT - LESSON OF MODERN WARFARE.

TWICE DAILY, at THREE AND EIGHT.
Admission, 1s. RESERVED SEATS, 2s., 3s., 3s.
CHILDREN under 10 years of age, HALF-PRICE TO ALL PARTS.

PRINCE OF WALES THEATRE BIRMINGHAM
PRICES OF ADMISSION

	STALLS		DRESS CIRCLE		UPPER CIRCLE		BALCONY
	6/-	4/-	3/-	5/6	4/6	3/6	2/6	1/-
REDUCED PRICE MATINEES	5/-	3/6	2/6	5/-	4/-	2/6	2/-	1/-

ALL SEATS NOW BOOKABLE IN ADVANCE

Box Office open daily from 10 to 10.   Phone MIDland 5684 (3 lines)

Please enclose stamped addressed envelope with enquiry for seats

The management reserve the right to make any alterations in the cast rendered necessary, owing to illness or other unavoidable causes.

1936

Prince of Wales Theatre,
BROAD STREET.

Tel. Address, "Theatrical."   Tel. No. 684.

To-night (Friday,) & To-morrow (Saturday,) at 7.30,

MICE AND MEN.

Monday Next, October 20,

MR. JOHN HARE.

Supported by
MISS FORTESCUE & POWERFUL COMPANY

Monday and Tuesday, "The Gay Lord Quex."
Wednesday, Thursday, and Thursday Matinée,
"A Pair of Spectacles,"
Friday and Saturday, "Caste"

October 27th, "BECKY SHARP."

Box Plans Open 9 to 5-30 Daily.

The Grand Theatre,
CORPORATION STREET, BIRMINGHAM
Telephone No. 267.

Last Two Nights at 7.30,

Mr. MILTON BODE'S COMPANY of 60 Artistes,
Including the Famous American Comedian,
Mr. TOM E. MURRAY, in

AN ENGLISH DAISY.

The old Birmingham Repertory Theatre, Station Street, November 1931.

Tivoli Theatre
HURST STREET, BIRMINGHAM.

TWO PERFORMANCES NIGHTLY at 7 & 9.

Monday Next and during the week,
Expensive Engagement of
EPH THOMPSON'S Wonderful Performing Elephants, including "Bill," the Soldier Elephant, First time in England.
LA BELLE WILMA, Sand and Smoke Painter,
MONS. SALAMONSKY and his Serpentine Dancing Horse,
AND STAR COMPANY.

Morning Performance, Thursday, October 23rd.

Note the Prices :—Gallery, 2d.; Pit, 4d.; Circle, 6d.; Stalls, 1s.; Boxes, per seat, 2s

---

TOWN HALL, BIRMINGHAM.

Thursday Evening, Oct. 30

Early Doors, 6-15 (for Ticket Holders.)
Commence at 7-30 p.m.

ONLY APPEARANCE THIS SEASON OF

KUBELIK.

Under the Management of

HUGO GÖRLITZ,
119, NEW BOND STREET, LONDON.

Aston Hippodrome, February 1958.

The last show at the Theatre Royal, New Street, December 1956. By coincidence, in 1975, Alton appeared as Principal Comic with the Fol-de-Rols at the De La Warr Pavilion, Bexhill-on-Sea.

A feature of the Alexandra Theatre pantomime season was always the presentation of a cake to the cast by Reg Wimbush of A.D. Wimbush & Son Ltd. Sandy Powell stands second left in this 1925 group.

Church of England Working Men's Society Band, Northfield School Yard, c. 1890.

Birmingham City Police Band, 1921.

Masque Ballroom, Walford Road, Sparkbrook, 1926.

The Bristol Cinema, Bristol Street, 1936.

Sid Field, theatre and film star, visits Osborn Road, Sparkbrook, where he was born. October 1946.

◁ *Tony Hancock, TV, stage and radio star, was born at 41, Southam Road, Hall Green on 12th May 1924.*

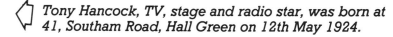

Morning inspection at the Paramount Theatre, New Street,(later the Odeon). It opened in September 1937, as part of a £750,000 development. Sadly it meant the demolition of the old King Edward's School.

This is how thousands of people will recall the Tatler, functioning in its heyday mainly as a cartoon theatre, 1937. Over the years it became the Select, the Tatler, the Jacey, the Classic and finally, today the dual Tivoli Cinemas.

7th May 1945

AMUSEMENTS

THEATRE ROYAL. MID. 4-3-5-5. D'OYLY CARTE OPERA COMPANY in Gilbert & Sullivan Operas. To-night & Tomorrow at 6.0: "The Yeoman of the Guard." Next Week: Webster Booth and Anne Zeigler in new musical romance, "Sweet Yesterday."

ALEXANDRA THEATRE.
Commencing Tuesday, May 8.
Evenings at 6.30.
Matinees Wednesday and Saturday, 2.30.
"THE LATE CHRISTOPHER BEAN."

REPERTORY THEATRE. Evenings (except Monday), 6. Matinees, Wednesday, Thursday, Saturday, 2, "SHE STOOPS TO CONQUER," by Oliver Goldsmith. May 15: "The Seagull," by Tchekov. Box Office 10.30—6.30. No Phone Bookings.

SHAKESPEARE Festival, Memorial Theatre, Stratford-on-Avon, March 31 to Sept. Evngs. 7.30; Mats. Weds. & Sats., 2.30. Resvd. seats 3/- to 8/6 can be booked at Dale, Forty & Co., 80, New St., Bham. (MID. 2251) or Box Office (Strat.-on-A. 2271). Open 10—8.

HIPPODROME, HURST STREET. 5.10, 7.25. Mats. Wed., Thur. Sat. 2.30. Tom Arnold's Big Top Circus. Lions, Tigers, Arab Horses, Seals, Monkeys, Dogs, Unridable Mules, Chinese Wonders, Equestrians, Acrobats, Trapezists, Jugglers, Aquatics, Famous Clowns.

ASTON HIPPODROME. AST. 0815. Box Office 10—5.30. This Week: 6.0 Twice Brightly, 8.0. RADIO VACATION. Morris & Cowley, Derek Roy, Peggy Ashley, Victor Seyforth, Peggy (Piano), Desmond, Two Valors, and Support.

DUDLEY HIPPODROME. 5.15 Twice Nightly 7.30. Syd Seymour with his Mad Hatters of 1945. The Bredwins, Constance Evans, Mad Hatters Band, Carvey & Mac, Alfred Thripp, Michael Roxy, Beau Peep Cuties. Next Week: "Appointment with Fear."

HIPPODROME, COVENTRY. Phone: 3141. THIS WEEK. Nightly 6 p.m. Mats. Wed., Thurs. & Sat. at 2.30. Harry Benet presents "BETTY," with Betty Leslie-Smith, Bertram Wallis, Reginald Palmer and FREDDIE FORBES.

FUTURIST THEATRE. TO-DAY: "JANIE" (U), featuring JOYCE REYNOLDS, ROBERT HUTTON, EDWARD ARNOLD, ANN HARDING. Rollicking Story! Non-stop Frolic! At 12.30, 2.55, 5.20, 7.45. And Full Programme.

SCALA, TO-DAY: RONALD COLMAN, KAY FRANCIS in "CYNARA" (A), 2, 4.55, 7.53; ELYSE KNOX, ANNE GILLIS, SALLY EILERS in "A WAVE, A WAC AND A MARINE" (U), 12.40, 3.35 and 6.30.

FORUM (A.B.C.). Cont. 1.5 p.m. Margaret O'Brien, June Allyson, Jimmy Durante, Jose Iturbi in "MUSIC FOR MILLIONS" (A), at 1.55, 4.40, 7.30. "A Picture in a Million." "GOING WYE WAY" (U), at 1.5, 3.50, 6.35.

GAUMONT. Continuous from 12.0. PAUL MUNI, MERLE OBERON, CORNEL WILDE, in "A SONG TO REMEMBER" (A) (Tech.). Screened at 12.10, 2.40, 5.10, 7.35 p.m. HUGH HERBERT in "OH! BABY" (A), at 2.5, 4.35, and 7.0 p.m.

WEST END (A G.-B. Theatre). Mid. 0022. Continuous from 12 noon. Donald O'Connor, Peggy Ryan, Jack Oakie in THE MERRY MONAHANS" (A), 1.30, 4.40, 7.50. Basil Rathbone, Nigel Bruce in "THE PEARL OF DEATH" (A), 12.10, 3.20, 6.30.

ODEON, New St. Cont. from 10 a.m. The Greatest Picture America Ever Made. "WILSON" (U), with Alexander Knox, Ruth Nelson, Geraldine Fitzgerald, Thomas Mitchell, Sir Cedric Hardwicke. At 10.55, 1.50, 4.40, 7.30. All Next Week: "Can't Help Singing."

MIDLAND JAZZ JAMBOREE
AT THE MIDLAND INSTITUTE,
ON WEDNESDAY, MAY 9th, at 6.30 p.m.
Tickets 4/6 and 3/6 from
ALAN G. PRIESTLEY,
27B, PARADISE STREET, BIRMINGHAM.

WRESTLING EVERY SATURDAY
NIGHT at 7 p.m.,
BIRMINGHAM STADIUM, GOSTA GREEN.
Popular Prices: 2/9 to 10/-.
Phone: AST. 5951.

NEWS THEATRE, HIGH STREET. 10.30 Daily. 10d. & 1/8 Only. Suns. 3.0 "TARAWA" (World-in-Action Series). "ON THE MELLOW SIDE" (Musical). New Disney Cartoon. Color. Travel. WORLD'S LATEST NEWS.

TATLER, STATION STREET. Cont 10.15 To-day. Prices 10d. & 1/8. "RUSSIAN SALAD" (introducing the Lenin State Orchestra); "Mackinac Island" (Coloured Travel); "Commando Duck" (Donald Duck); "Past Performances" (Sports); LATEST NEWS

THE MASQUE
Birmingham's Best Ballroom.
Open Daily 3—5.45, & 6.45 to 10 p.m.
Every Thursday 50/50 Old-Time & Modn. Dance under the direction of H. Gilliver, I.D.M.A.
VIC. 1397. Walford Road, Sparkbrook.

BENTLEY-WALL DANCES, ACOCKS GREEN PUBLIC HALL. MON. 7.30—10.30, 2/-. RIPS ASTORIAS. WED., First Heat of Trophy Contest for Couples never placed in Rec. Championship. Demonstration by SIMPSON & KRAUTH.

BERT NEILSON SCHOOL OF DANCING.
PARAMOUNT.
Beginners or Otherwise.
LYNDHURST, LLOYD ST., SMALL HEATH.
Phone: VIC. 2849.

BIRMINGHAM'S Finest Studio.
THE WATTS & BILLY KNEE.
MONDAY, 7.30 to 10, Tuition 2/-
WEDNESDAY, 7.30 to 10, Tuition 2/-
THURSDAY, 7.30 to 10, Medal Class ... 2/6
Over Burton's, top of Bull Ring. Mid. 1731.

CRYSTAL PALACE BALLROOM,
SUTTON PARK, SUTTON COLDFIELD.
DANCING EVERY
MON., 2/- WED., 2/- FRI., 2/- SAT., 3/-
TEDDY THOMAS and His Ballroom Orchestra.

FRANK DOCKER
FOR
PRIVATE DANCING LESSONS.
QUEEN'S COLLEGE CHAMBERS,
PARADISE ST. MID. 2161. 10 a.m.—9 p.m.

GEORGE RAY'S Dancing Academy, 537, COVENTRY RD., SMALL HEATH. Mon., Wed. and Fri., Beginners' Instruction, 7.30 till 10, 1/6; Mon. Afternoon, 3 till 5, 50/50, 9d.; Sat., Advanced Practice, 7.30 till 10.30, 2/-; Special Class Victory Night.

GOODALL'S POPULAR DANCES.
MONDAYS & WEDNESDAYS,
7.30-10.30, 1/6. SATURDAYS,
SUPER NIGHTS, 6.30-10.30, 2/6.
ST. PAUL'S BALLROOM, BALSALL HEATH.
St. Paul's Rd. off Moseley Rd. 41, 42 Tram.

GRAND CASINO,
CORPORATION STREET.
MECCA DANCING
At 2.30 and 6.30.
TWICE DAILY.

PRIVATE LESSONS DAILY. Phone: MID. 6607. We lead, others follow. We gave you BEGINNERS ONLY, and now MONDAYS CONTINENTAL NIGHT. DIPPNALL SCHOOL OF DANCING, 38, John Bright Street (corner Station St.).

SPRINGFIELD BALLROOM,
corner Solihull Rd. & Stratford Rd.
NON-STOP DANCING EVERY NIGHT.
TO-NIGHT, 7.30—10.30.
VE-DAY: SPECIAL DANCE—
Non-Stop Dancing 7 till 12 (midnight).

TUESDAYS YOU DANCE
With All Your Friends and
RONNIE HANCOX WITH HIS BAND,
8—11 p.m. Admission 3/-.
THE GEORGE HOTEL,
SOLIHULL'S DANCE FOR DANCERS.

TUESDAY, BEGINNERS' CLASS.
AUTHENTIC BALLROOM DANCING,
7.30—10, CO-OP. 386, STRATFORD ROAD
(by Piccadilly Cinema), SPARKHILL.
Modern Qualified Teachers.
JIMMY & LOLA CLARK, N.A.T.D., M.A.T.D.

TOWN HALL DANCES
AS USUAL.
WEDNESDAYS, May 9 and 16. SATURDAYS, May 12 and 19.

ICE SKATING RINK,
SUMMER HILL ROAD. CEN. 6036.
THREE SESSIONS DAILY:
11 a.m., 2.30 p.m. and 6.30 p.m.

CINEMATOGRAPH EXHIBITORS' ASSOCIATION

Usual Times of Opening: Week-days, 2 p.m.—10.30 p.m.; Sundays, 3 p.m.—9 p.m.
Houses marked * den otes six-day programme.

ADELPHI, Hay Mills (A.B.C.). Belita, "Lady Let's Dance" (U); David Niven, "Eternally Yours" (A).

ALBION*—"Double Indemnity" (A) "Caribbean Romance" (U). Sun.: "Let George Do It" (U), "Fangs of the Wild" (A).

ALHAMBRA, Moseley Rd. (A.B.C.). Anton Walbrook, Sally Gray, "Dangerous Moonlight" (U); "The Contender" (A).

APOLLO, Tyburn Road.—Margaret Lockwood, "Love Story" (U). Fine Supporting Prog. Thurs.: "Fiddlers Three" (A).

ASTORIA, Aston * (A.B.C.).— George Formby, "He Snoops to Conquer" (U); Tom Neal, Two-Man Submarine (A).

ATLAS.—Richard Arlen, Erich von Stroheim, "Storm Over Lisbon" (A). Ruth Terry, "Sing Neighbour Sing" (U).

AVION, Aldridge. ALD. 52312. Judy Garland, "Little Nellie Kelly" (U), 3.38, 6.11, 8.44. Full Support.

BEACON, Great Barr.—"Bulldog Drummond Strikes Back" (A), "My Gal Loves Music" (U). Thurs.: "The Climax" (A).

BEACON, Smethwick (A.B.C.).— Rita Hayworth, Gene Kelly, "Cover Girl" (U), Tech.; Latest News; Sup. Prog.

BEAUFORT * — Phyllis Calvert, "Madonna of the Seven Moons" (A). Sunday: "Man Who Lost Himself" (U).

BIRCHFIELD.—Pat O'Brien, Robt. Ryan, "Marine Raiders" (A); "Passport to Destiny" (A). Thurs.: "2,000 Women" (A).

BRISTOL, Bristol Road * (A.B.C.). Joan Fontaine, Arturo de Cordova, "FRENCHMAN'S CREEK" (A), Tech.

BROADWAY. MID. 1761. Fredric March, "ADVENTURES OF MARK TWAIN" (U). Supporting Programme.

CAPITOL.—Frank Sinatra, George Murphy, "Step Lively" (U); Peter Lorre in "Face Behind the Mask" (A).

CARLTON. SOU. 0861.—Pat O'Brien, "Marine Raiders" (A) · "Find the Blackmailer" A. Thurs.: "Virginia City" U.

CASTLE Bromwich Cinema. CAS. 2425 Boris Karloff, Susanna Foster in "The Climax" (A), Tech. Full Supp. Programme.

CLIFTON, Great Barr. Katharine Hepburn, Walter Huston in "DRAGON SEED" (A), 2.25, 5.10, 7.55.

CORONET.—Gail Russell, Diana Lynn, "Our Hearts Were Young and Gay" (U); "Meet Sexton Blake" (A).

CROWN, Ladywood * (A.B.C.).— Joan Fontaine, Basil Rathbone, "FRENCHMAN'S CREEK" (A), Tech.

DANILO, Longbridge. — Felix Aylmer, "Mr. Emmanuel" (A), 2.5, 5.0, 8.10. "The Falcon in Mexico" (A), 3.50, 6.40.

DANILO, Quinton.—"Gypsy Wild-cat" (Tech.), 3.28, 5.59, 8.35; "Moon Over Las Vegas," 2.10, 4.41, 7.17.

EDGBASTON, Monument Road.* (A.B.C.). R. Colman, M. Dietrich, "Kismet" (U) (Tech.); "St. Paul's Cathedral" (U).

ELITE, H'worth * — John Mills, Stewart Granger, "Waterloo Road" (A); "Reckless Age" (U).

EMPRESS, Sutton (A.B.C.).— Bing Crosby, "ROAD TO MOROCCO" (U); "TWO MAN SUBMARINE" (A).

ERA, Bordesley Green. VIC. 0543. Robert Newton in "THIS HAPPY BREED" (A). Also Full Support.

GAIETY, Coleshill Street (A.B.C.).— Belita, "LADY LET'S DANCE" (U); Bruce Bennett, "DANGEROUS MISTS" (A).

GRAND, Soho Road. "FOLLOW THE BOYS" (U), George Raft, Vera Zorina, and Full Support.

GRANGE. — Ann Sothern, John Hodiak, "You Can't Do That to Me" (A); Jimmy Lydon, "Henry Boy Scout" (U).

GROVE * — "Frenchman's Creek" A (Tech.). Mon. to Fri. 2.54, 5.26, 7.58. Sat. 5.7, 7.37. Sun.: "Young in Heart" (U).

IMPERIAL, Moseley Road (A.B.C.). Vera Lynn, Donald Stewart, "One Exciting Night" (A); "Gamblers Choice" (A).

KING'S NORTON. KIN. 1079.— Jean Arthur, Lee Bowman, "The Impatient Years" (U); "South of Dixie" (U).

KINGSTON.—Vera Ralston, Eric Stroheim, "Storm Over Lisbon" (A); Ruth Tarry, "Sing Neighbour, Sing" (U).

KINGSWAY * HIG. 1352. "Frenchman's Creek" (A), Joan Fontaine, Arturo De Cordova. Sun.: "The Squeaker" (A).

LYRIC. — Bing Crosby, Dorothy Lamour, "The Road To Morocco". (U), etc. Thurs.: "The Climax" (A) (Tech.).

LUXOR,—Paul Lukas, Carl Esmond "Address Unknown" (A); "The Scarlet Claw" A. Thurs.: "Adam Had Four Sons" A.

MAJESTIC, Smethwick.— Pat O'Brien, Robert Ryan, Ruth Hussey, "Marine Raiders" (A); "Texas Kid" (U).

MAYPOLE. WAR. 2051.—Spencer Tracy, Signe Hasso, "Seventh Cross" (A), 2.50, 5.15, 7.45. Also Full Support.

MOSELEY PICTURE HOUSE.— Robert Lowery, "HOT RHYTHM" (U); "CALL OF THE JUNGLE" (A).

NORTHFIELD CINEMA. PRI. 1406. Katharine Hepburn, Walter Huston in "DRAGON SEED" (A), 4.45, 7.30 approx.

OAK, Selly Oak * (A.B.C.).— Phyllis Calvert, Stewart Granger, "MADONNA OF THE SEVEN MOONS" (A).

ODEON, Black Heath. Warner Baxter, Ingrid Bergman, "Adam Had Four Sons" (A); "Nine Girls" (A).

ODEON, Shirley * Cont. 1.40—10. "Frenchman's Creek" (A) & supp. prog. Sunday (4): "Journey Into Fear" (A) Etc.

**ODEON, Warley *** P. Calvert, S. Granger in "Madonna of the Seven Moons" (A), at 2.30, 5.15, 8.0.

OLTON.—Belita, James Ellison, "Lady, Let's Dance" (U); Miriam Hopkins in "Woman Chases Man" (U).

ORIENT, Aston * (A.B.C.).— Brian Donlevy, "An American Romance" (U), Tech. "Father Is a Prince" (A).

PALACE, Erdington * (A.B.C.).— Merle Oberon, "Dark Waters" (A); Chas. Boyer, "History Is Made At Night" (A).

PALLADIUM, Hockley (A.B.C.).— Alice Faye, "Little Old New York" (U); Billy Scott, "A Night of Magic" (A).

PAVILION, Stirchley * (A.B.C.). Brian Donlevy, "An American Romance" (U), Tech.; "Father Is a Prince" (A).

PAVILION, Wylde Green * (ABC). Brian Donlevy, "An American Romance" (U), Tech.; "Father Is a Prince" (A).

PICTURE House, Harborne (G.-B.). Har. 1281. "Madonna of the Seven Moons." 2.10, 5.0, 7.45 (A); "Toscanini" (U).

PICCADILLY, Sparkbrook * (ABC) Joan Fontaine, Arturo de Cordova, "Frenchman's Creek" (A), Tech.

PLAZA, Stockland Gn. Daily 2—10. "Step Lively" (A), "'Neath Brooklyn Bridge" (A). Thurs.: "Marine Raiders" (A).

REGAL, Handsworth * (A.B.C.).— Brian Donlevy, "An American Romance" (U) (Tech.); "Father is a Prince" (A).

RIALTO, Hall Green. SPR. 1270.— "They Came to a City" (U), Googie Withers, J. Clements; "The Chinese Cat" (A).

RINK, Smethwick * (G.-B.). 2—10. SME. 0950. "Summer Storm" (A), 2.5, 5.0, 7.50. "Our Mr. Shakespeare" (U).

RITZ, Bordesley Green E. (A.B.C.). Belita, "LADY LET'S DANCE" (U); David Niven, "ETERNALLY YOURS" (A).

ROBIN HOOD, Hall Green * (ABC) Brian Donlevy, "An American Romance" (U) (Tech.); "Father is a Prince" (A).

ROCK, Alum Rock.—June Haver, "Irish Eyes Are Smiling" (U) (Tech.); "Sons of the Air" U. Thur. "Beloved Enemy" A

ROOKERY, Handsworth. Phyllis Calvert, Flora Robson, "2,000 Women" (A); "So's Your Uncle" (U).

ROYALTY, Harborne * (A.B.C.).— Ronald Colman, Marlene Dietrich, "KISMET" (U) (Tech.). Full supporting prog.

RUBERY CINEMA. RUBERY 193. "One Exciting Night" (A); "Towpath" (U). Thurs.: "Old Mother Riley Overseas" (U)

SHELDON—"The Secret Command" (A); "Meet Sexton Blake" (A). Thurs.: "Waterloo Road" (A).

SOLIHULL. SOL. 0398.—Franchot Tone, Veronica Lake, "Hour Before the Dawn" (A). Thurs.: "Holiday Inn" (U).

STAR.—"Whistling in Brooklyn" (A), Red Skelton and Ann Rutherford, at 3.25, 5.40 and 8.0.

TIVOLI. — "In Society" (U); "Pardon My Rhythm" (A). Sunday: "Corregidor" (A), "Follies Girl" (U).

TUDOR, King's Heath (A.B.C.).— Dorothy Lamour, "Rainbow Island" (U). (Tech.). Tom Neal, "Klondike Kate" (A).

TYSELEY CINEMA. ACO. 0133. "The Hitler Gang" (A), Robert Watson; "Take It Big" (U), Jack Haley.

VICTORIA. EAS. 0479.—"Marine Raiders" (A); "Pistol Packin' Mamma" (A). Thurs.: "Storm Over Lisbon" (A).

VILLA CROSS* (G.-B.). NOR. 0607. Geo. Sanders, "Summer Storm" (A); "Gamblers Choice" (A). Sun. "First Love" (U).

WEOLEY— "Escape from Crime" (A); "She Couldn't Say No" (U). Thurs. "Lady Let's Dance" (U).

WINDSOR, Smethwick*—"French-man's Creek" (A) (Tech.); "Eagle Versus Dragon" U. Sun. (6), Gentleman After Dark A.

WINSON GREEN Picture Palace. "Action in Arabia" (A), Geo. Sanders. Thurs.: "Hey Rookie" (U), Ann Miller.

The Night Out dancers, Horse Fair, March 1976. The nightclub opened in 1975 and became the Dome ten years later.

GREEN & PLEASANT

Remembering that Birmingham originally consisted of twelve ancient parishes, it is easy to appreciate that most of the present city's outlying districts were themselves once villages or hamlets and formed part of England's green and pleasant land.

Kings Norton annually held its Mop Fair on the Green on the first Monday in October from as early as the 17th century. There were roundabouts, stalls, side-shows and ox-roasts. Young men and women paraded with mops and buckets or with other tools of their trade and offered themselves for employment. The Mop, in a revised form, still takes place to this day.

In the early 1900's Selly Oak was a peaceful, tree-lined village with its cottages, shops, marble horse-trough, and local inn, "The Oak", whose licensee, 'Hawk-eye' Lilley, was the famous Warwickshire and England wicket-keeper.

There were 330 acres taken into care by the Bournville Village Trust late in 1900 and by 1955 there were 3,500 dwellings housing 11,000 people. The village typified controlled urban development, carefully laid out to capitalise on open space and so preserve a semi-rural atmosphere.

The rural Edgbaston of 1831 attracted to its Botanical Gardens large attendances on "People's Days" (Mondays), with Flower Shows offering valuable prizes eagerly contested for by numerous horticulturists and florists in Birmingham and its neighbourhood. Rhododendron beds appeared in 1838, a lily-house in 1851, in 1871 a palm-house, and a rock-garden in 1895. Even a laughing jackass (a kingfisher-type bird) was introduced in 1913.

Our modern "Shard End" derives from a "sherd" or "shard" which was a detached, isolated or intrusive portion of a manor -in this case, Castle Bromwich.

Off-duty gardeners pose with grim determination in the grounds of the Botanical Gardens, c. 1895.

The Botanical Gardens, Edgbaston, August 1951.

Longbridge Lane, near the present site of the Railway Station, September 1922. The Austin is on the left.

The Old Quarry, Weoley Castle, March 1935. This area is now part of Jervoise Road Recreation Ground.

Pershore Road South, Kings Norton, 1930.

Moor Green Lane, Moseley, taken from the corner of Yew Tree Road in the direction of Russell Road, 1932.

Up the hill to Cotteridge. The same area, as above, after the road had been widened, August 1932.

Moseley, looking west along Salisbury Road, 1952. Taken fro the tower of the Parish Church.

836, Stratford Road, Sparkhill, c. 1950.

Billesley Farm, c. 1895.

Happy Valley, a popular leisure area, Yardley Wood, c. 1913.

Old cottages in Fox Hollies Road, Hall Green, shortly before demolition for road-widening, November 1938.

Hobmoor Road, Small Heath, 1910.

Coventry Road, with Arden Oak Road on the left, Sheldon, c. 1950.

Tile Cross Inn (near Sheldon Hall), 1896.

Perry Common Road, March 1925.

*Stechford Road, with Hodgehill Common on the l[...]
November 1933.*

Warren Farm Estate, Kingstanding, September 1929.

Manwoods Farm, The Uplands, Handsworth, c. 1910.

Church Lane, Handsworth, October 1956.

Handsworth Park. 1910.

Preparations for the boating season at Cannon Hill Park, March 1952.

Hall of Memory, Broad Street, 1963.

ACKNOWLEDGEMENTS

(for providing photographs, for encouragement and numerous other favours)

Balsall Heath Library; Birmingham Mint plc.; Birmingham Post and Mail Staff; Birmingham Reference Library, Local Studies; Nell Blackburn; Blue Coat School; Charlie Bottrill; Boys' Brigade; Len Bracey; British Red Cross Society, West Midlands; British Waterways Board, Amenities Services Division; John Brown; Cadbury Schweppes Ltd.; Rev Michael Caddy; Arthur Camwell; Dave and Kath Carpenter; Castle Vale Library; Leslie Checkley; Children's Hospital; Edna Davis; Leslie Deakins; Rosalind Dickers; Shirley Dillon; Fred Dorrell; Federation of Boys' Clubs; First Leisure Corporation; Francis and Eva Franks; Girl Guides' Association; Glebe Farm Library; Arthur Gossage Ltd.; Reg and Doreen Gower; Barry Griffiths; Handsworth Historical Society; Clive Hardy; Head Postmaster, Birmingham; Albert Hughes; Anne Jennings; Dave and Thelma Jones; Mabel Judd; Edith Kemp; Hazel Kennedy; Kings Norton Library; Kings Norton Post Office; Kingstanding Library; Grace Lashford; Jack Malkin; John Markham; Denis and Mollie Martineau; Midland History Resources Centre, Newman College; Barbara Millington; Lily Moody; Moseley Football Club; Northfield Library; John O'Keeffe; Maurice and Gwen Price; Victor and Veronica Price; Quinton Library; R.S.P.C.A.; Joe Russell; St Benedict's Junior and Infant School; St John Ambulance, West Midlands County; Derek Salberg; Mary Sargeant; Scout Association; Selly Oak Hospital; Bill Shutts; Small Heath Library; Small Heath Local History Society; Stanley Smelt; Smith and Nephew Consumer Products Ltd.; Doris Spencer; Geraldine Spink; Stirchley Junior and Infant School; Gordon Stretch; Joe Sutton; Tower Hill Library; Connie Towle; Kath Watts; Dave Webb; West Heath Hospital; West Midlands Fire Service; Bob and Joan Wilkes; Rosemary Wilkes; Violet Winwood; Colin Woodhall; Winnie Wort; Stanley Wyton.

Please forgive any possible omissions. Every effort has been made to include all organisations and individuals involved in the book.

Alton's Books – so Far!

"BIRMINGHAM IN THE FIFTIES"
"BIRMINGHAM IN THE SIXTIES"
"BIRMINGHAM: A LOOK BACK"
"BIRMINGHAM REMEMBERED"
"MEMORIES OF BIRMINGHAM"
"BIRMINGHAM AT PLAY"
"BIRMINGHAM SHOPS"
"BIRMINGHAM AT WORK"
"BIRMINGHAM: THE WAR YEARS"
"BIRMINGHAM AT WAR VOL 1"
"BIRMINGHAM AT WAR VOL 2"
"DOGS IN BIRMINGHAM"
"COVENTRY: A CENTURY OF NEWS"
"MEMORIES OF COVENTRY"
"COVENTRY AT WAR"
"MEMORIES OF STRATFORD-UPON-AVON"
"JOE RUSSELL'S SMETHWICK"
"THE BLACK COUNTRY REMEMBERED"
"MEMORIES OF THE BLACK COUNTRY"
"THE BLACK COUNTRY AT PLAY"
"THE BLACK COUNTRY AT WAR"
"MEMORIES OF DUDLEY"
"MEMORIES OF WALSALL"
"MEMORIES OF WEST BROMWICH"
"MEMORIES OF WOLVERHAMPTON"
"MEMORIES OF SHREWSBURY"
"MEMORIES OF THE WREKIN AND BEYOND"
'ALTON DOUGLAS'S CELEBRITY RECIPES'
'ALTON DOUGLAS'S KNOW YOUR PLACE'

Contact leading booksellers or for ORDER FORM please write to:

Alton Douglas, c/o Brewin Books Ltd., Doric House, Church Street, Studley, Warwickshire B80 7LG.

ISBN 0-947731-81-4

9 780947 731816

£7.99

(Nett U.K. on